FREE FROM THE PAST

Bible Promises for Adult Children of Alcoholics

Compiled by
Gary Wilde

A
JANET
THOMA
BOOK

Thomas Nelson Publishers
Nashville

Published in Nashville, Tennessee, by Thomas
Nelson, Inc., and distributed in Canada by Lawson
Falle, Ltd., Cambridge, Ontario.

Scripture quotations are from the NEW KING JAMES
VERSION of the Bible. Copyright © 1979, 1980, 1982,
Thomas Nelson, Inc., Publishers.

Library of Congress Cataloging-in-Publication Data

Wilde, Gary.
    Free from the past / compiled by Gary Wilde.
        p.   cm. — (New perspectives)
    ISBN 0-8407-3244-9 (pbk.)
    1. Adult children of alcoholics—Prayer-books and
devotions—English.   I. Title.   II. Series.
BV4596.A48W55   1991
242'.4—dc20   92–3620
                                                    CIP
        Printed in the United States of America
            1 2 3 4 5 6 7 — 96 95 94 93 92

CONTENTS

THE PAST

1. Home: Did You Play the Enabler in a Dysfunctional Family? 3

Playing the Martyr: Martha Sacrifices, Feels Sorry for Herself • Playing the Rescuer: Joseph 'Saves' His Family • Playing the Placater: Reuben Tries to Smooth Things Over • Playing the Persecutor: Adam and Eve Cast Blame • Playing the Victim: Laborers Claim Unfairness

2. Parents: Did You Miss Out on Parental Care? 21

Did Your Parents Fail to Meet Their Responsibilities? • Will You Look to God for Reparenting? • Do You Recognize Your Responsibilities as a Child?

3. Abuse: Did You Suffer Emotional or Physical Wounds? 37

Facing the Pain of Abuse • Finding the Comfort of God • Freeing Myself from the Past

THE PRESENT

4. Emotions: Can You Learn to Live with Your Feelings?   59

Feeling Abandoned by Parents and God?
• . . . God Hears the Cry of the Abandoned
• Feeling Anxious and Worried? • . . . Give
Your Worries to God • Feeling Fearful?
• . . . Meet Fear with Divine Courage
• Holding in Anger? • . . . Express Anger
Properly • Feel Like a Failure? • . . . God
Promises Success through Obedience
• Having Feelings of Despair? • . . . God
Saves Us from Despair • Feeling Ashamed?
• . . . God Replaces Shame with Joy
• Experiencing Grief? • . . . Seek God's
Comfort in Grief • . . . And Remember:
God Promises an End to Sorrow and Death

5. Self-Esteem: Can You Change Your Self-Image?   77

Seeing My True Worth • Seeing Myself
through God's Eyes • Seeing My Life
through Good Self-Esteem

6. Accountability: Can You Uphold Your New Responsibilities?   92

The Requirements • My Responsibilities
• God's Response

THE FUTURE

7. Higher Power: Will You Look to God for Strength?   111

The 'Unknown God': The One So Close to Us • The Father: The One Who Made Us • The Son: The One Who Lived on Earth With Us • The Holy Spirit: The One Who Dwells Inside Us

8. Spiritual Life: Will You Seek New Avenues of Nurture?   130

Ask God for Vibrant Spiritual Life • Take Up the Challenge of the Spiritual Life • Rest in God's Inner Peace • Resist

9. Freedom: Will You Continue to Take Care of Yourself?   145

Taking Care of Myself • Setting New Personal Boundaries • Looking to the Future

10. Carrying the Recovery Message to Others   159

Thanking God for My Own 'Spiritual Awakening' • Befriending Those Looking for What's Missing •Offering the New Life to Others, through My 'Walk' • Offering the New Life to Others, through My Words

Index   180

Other Books in the New Perspective™ Series

Healing for Today, Hope for Tomorrow
Bible Promises for Overcoming Codependency
Hope for the Hungry Heart
Bible Promises for Overeaters
Renewed Each Day
Bible Promises for Overcoming Chemical Dependency

Introduction

As an adult child of an alcoholic, you experienced powerlessness over someone else's addiction. You learned behaviors that helped you survive, make it through each day. You played the martyr or the rescuer or the victim. You suffered emotional wounds that may now be buried so deep you don't even recognize them. You can take the first step toward serenity with *Free from the Past*.

A collection of Scripture passages from the New King James Version of the Bible, *Free from the Past* offers God's comfort and encouragement as you explore the issues related to your past abuse and begin your recovery. In the following pages you will discover the healing offered by a safe and loving Parent, "a father of the fatherless" (Psalm 68:5). You will begin to understand and freely experience your feelings and emotions and gain the strength you need to care for yourself emotionally and spiritually.

Free from the Past is arranged topically in

three sections—The Past, The Present, and The Future—so you can walk through the steps of your recovery as you read through this book from the first to the last page. Or you may choose to read and meditate on selected passages, focusing for a time on a specific aspect of your recovery.

You will walk with a new perspective through today and into the future as you are set free by God's words in *Free from the Past*.

THE
PAST

Home: Did You Play the Enabler in a Dysfunctional Family?

When we grow up in a dysfunctional family, we take on a role to play. Not that the role is directly assigned, or consciously accepted. Rather, it is assumed. Taking such roles is a way for the whole family to avoid direct confrontation of problems, and to avoid relating intimately with one another. It's also a way for family members to "protect" those suffering from alcoholic addiction.

Usually, the children in such families play an "enabling" role, such as: martyr (the one who sacrifices time, energy, and happiness to keep the family together), rescuer (the one who solves family problems and tries to "fix" painful situations), placater (the smooth talker who tries to keep family fights from erupting), persecutor (the one who "helps" the family by announcing who is to blame for family pain), or victim (the self-pitier who "takes the fall" for family troubles). What was your special role in your family of origin? How did your role help keep the peace? In what ways did it serve to keep you surviving?

Be thankful for the part your role served in protecting you from deeper emotional suffering. Playing that role was the best way you, a child, knew how to survive and maintain sanity in a world of adults out of control. But now you are ready to recover, to make some attempts at breaking out of the role-playing behaviors you've carried into your own adult life. Blessings upon you as you find the promises of Scripture leading you to new levels of wholeness!

Playing the Martyr: Martha Sacrifices, Feels Sorry for Herself

Now it happened as they went that He entered a certain village; and a certain woman named Martha welcomed Him into her house. And she had a sister called Mary, who also sat at Jesus' feet and heard His word. But Martha was distracted with much serving, and she approached Him and said, "Lord, do You not care that my sister has left me to serve alone? Therefore tell her to help me." And Jesus answered and said to her, "Martha, Martha, you are worried and troubled about many things. But one thing is needed, and Mary has chosen that good part, which will not be taken away from her."

—LUKE 10:38–42

■ God, the One Who Receives Unselfish Sacrifice

"Which of the prophets did your fathers not persecute? And they killed those who foretold the coming of the Just One, of whom you now have become the betrayers and murderers, who have received the law by the direction of angels and have not kept it." When they heard these things they were cut to the heart, and they gnashed at him with their teeth. But he, being full of the Holy Spirit, gazed into heaven and saw the glory of God, and Jesus standing at the right hand of God, and said, "Look! I see the heavens opened and the Son of Man standing at the right hand of God!" Then they cried out with a loud voice, stopped their ears, and ran at him with one accord; and they cast him out of the city and stoned him. And the witnesses laid down their clothes at the feet of a young man named Saul. And they stoned Stephen as he was calling on God and saying, "Lord Jesus, receive my spirit."

—ACTS 7:52–59

Playing the Rescuer: Joseph 'Saves' His Family

And Joseph situated his father and his brothers, and gave them a possession in the land of Egypt, in the best of the land, in the land of Rameses, as Pharaoh had commanded. Then Joseph provided his father, his brothers, and all his father's household with bread, according to the number in their families. . . . And Joseph gathered up all the money that was found in the land of Egypt and in the land of Canaan, for the grain which they bought; and Joseph brought the money into Pharaoh's house. . . . Then Joseph said to the people, "Indeed I have bought you and your land this day for Pharaoh. Look, here is seed for you, and you shall sow the land." . . . So they said, "You have saved our lives. . . . "

—GENESIS 47:11–12, 14, 23, 25a

■ *God, the One Who Rescues and Saves Eternally*

Therefore say to the children of Israel: "I am the LORD; I will bring you out from under the burdens of the Egyptians, I will rescue you from their bondage, and I will redeem you with an outstretched arm and with great judgments."

—EXODUS 6:6

The LORD is my light and my salvation;
Whom shall I fear?
The LORD is the strength of my life;
Of whom shall I be afraid?
When the wicked came against me
To eat up my flesh,
My enemies and foes,
They stumbled and fell.

Though an army should encamp against me,
My heart shall not fear;
Though war should rise against me,
In this I will be confident.
One thing I have desired of the LORD,
That will I seek:
That I may dwell in the house of the LORD
All the days of my life,
To behold the beauty of the LORD,
And to inquire in His temple.
For in the time of trouble
He shall hide me in His pavilion;
In the secret place of His tabernacle
He shall hide me;
He shall set me high upon a rock.

—PSALM 27:1–5

For this is good and acceptable in the sight of God our Savior, who desires all men to be saved and to come to the knowledge of the truth. . . . This is a faithful saying and worthy of all acceptance. For to this end we both labor and suffer reproach, because we trust in the living God, who is the Savior of all men, especially of those who believe.

—1 TIMOTHY 2:3–4, 9–10

But when the kindness and the love of God our Savior toward man appeared, not by works of righteousness which we have done, but according to His mercy He saved us, through the washing of regeneration and renewing of the Holy Spirit, whom He poured out on us abundantly through Jesus Christ our Savior.

—TITUS 3:4–6

And you He made alive, who were dead in trespasses and sins, in which you once walked according to the course of this world, according to the prince of the power of the air, the spirit who now works in the sons of disobedience, among whom also we all once conducted ourselves in the lusts of our flesh, fulfilling the desires of the flesh and of the mind, and were by nature children of wrath, just as the others. But God, who is rich in mercy, because of His great love with which He loved us, even when we were dead in trespasses, made us alive together with Christ (by grace you have been saved), and raised us up together, and made us sit together in the heavenly places in Christ Jesus, that in the ages to come He might show the exceeding riches of His grace in His kindness toward us in Christ Jesus. For by grace you have been saved through faith, and that not of yourselves; it is the gift of God, not of works, lest anyone should boast.

—EPHESIANS 2:1–9

Playing the Placater: Reuben Tries to Smooth Things Over

Now Joseph dreamed, and he told it to his brothers; and they hated him even more. So he said to them, "Please hear this dream which I have dreamed: There we were, binding sheaves in the field. Then behold, my sheaf arose and also stood upright; and indeed your sheaves stood all around and bowed down to my sheaf." And his brothers said to him, "Shall you indeed reign over us? Or shall you indeed have dominion over us?" So they hated him even more for his dreams and for his words. . . . And his brothers envied him, but his father kept the matter in mind.

Then his brothers went to feed their father's flock in Shechem. And Israel said to Joseph, "Are not your brothers feeding the flock in Shechem? Come, I will send you to them." So he said to him, "Here I am." Then he said to him, "Please go and see if it is well with your brothers and well with the flocks, and bring back word to me." So he sent him out of the Valley of Hebron, and he went to Shechem. . . .

Now when they saw him afar off, even before he came near them, they conspired against him to kill him. Then they said to one another, "Look, this dreamer is coming! Come therefore, let us now kill him and cast him into some pit; and we shall say, 'Some wild beast has devoured him.' We shall see what will become of his dreams!"

But Reuben heard it, and he delivered him out of their hands, and said, "Let us not kill him." And Reuben said to them, "Shed no blood, but cast him into this pit which is in the wilderness, and do not lay a hand on him"—that he might deliver him out of their hands, and bring him back to his father.

So it came to pass, when Joseph had come to his brothers, that they stripped Joseph of his tunic, the tunic of many colors that was on him. Then they took him and cast him into a pit. And the pit was empty; there was no water in it. . . .

Then Midianite traders passed by; so the brothers pulled Joseph up and lifted him out of the pit, and sold him to the Ishmaelites for twenty shekels of silver. And they took Joseph to Egypt. Then Reuben returned to the pit, and indeed Joseph was not in the pit; and he tore his clothes. And he returned to his brothers and said, "The lad is no more; and I, where shall I go?"

—GENESIS 37:5–8, 11–14, 18–24, 28–30

■ *God, the One Who Smooths, Calms, and Reconciles*

"Comfort, yes, comfort My people!"
Says your God.
"Speak comfort to Jerusalem, and cry out to
    her,
That her warfare is ended,
That her iniquity is pardoned;
For she has received from the LORD's hand
Double for all her sins."
The voice of one crying in the wilderness:
"Prepare the way of the LORD;
Make straight in the desert
A highway for our God.
Every valley shall be exalted

And every mountain and hill be made low;
The crooked places shall be made straight,
And the rough places smooth."

—ISAIAH 40:1–4

On the same day, when evening had come, He said to them, "Let us cross over to the other side." Now when they had left the multitude, they took Him along in the boat as He was. And other little boats were also with Him. And a great windstorm arose, and the waves beat into the boat, so that it was already filling. But He was in the stern, asleep on a pillow. And they awoke Him and said to Him, "Teacher, do You not care that we are perishing?" Then He arose and rebuked the wind, and said to the sea, "Peace, be still!" And the wind ceased and there was a great calm. But He said to them, "Why are you so fearful? How is it that you have no faith?" And they feared exceedingly, and said to one another, "Who can this be, that even the wind and the sea obey Him!"

—MARK 4:35–41

Now all things are of God, who has reconciled us to Himself through Jesus Christ, and has given us the ministry of reconciliation, that is, that God was in Christ reconciling the world to Himself, not imputing their trespasses to them, and has committed to us the word of reconciliation. Therefore, we are ambassadors for Christ, as though God were pleading through us: we implore you on

Christ's behalf, be reconciled to God. For He made Him who knew no sin to be sin for us, that we might become the righteousness of God in Him.

—2 CORINTHIANS 5:18–21

Playing the Persecutor: Adam and Eve Cast Blame

Now the serpent was more cunning than any beast of the field which the LORD God had made. And he said to the woman, "Has God indeed said, 'You shall not eat of every tree of the garden'?"

And the woman said to the serpent, "We may eat the fruit of the trees of the garden; but of the fruit of the tree which is in the midst of the garden, God has said, 'You shall not eat it, nor shall you touch it, lest you die.'"

And the serpent said to the woman, "You will not surely die. For God knows that in the day you eat of it your eyes will be opened, and you will be like God, knowing good and evil."

So when the woman saw that the tree was good for food, that it was pleasant to the eyes, and a tree desirable to make one wise, she took of its fruit and ate. She also gave to her husband with her, and he ate. Then the eyes of both of them were opened, and they knew that they were naked; and they sewed fig leaves together and made themselves coverings. And they heard the sound of the LORD God walking in the garden in the cool of the day, and Adam and his wife hid themselves from the presence of the LORD God among the trees of the garden.

Then the LORD God called to Adam and said to him, "Where are you?"

So he said, "I heard Your voice in the garden, and I was afraid because I was naked; and I hid myself."

And He said, "Who told you that you were naked? Have you eaten from the tree of which I commanded you that you should not eat?"

Then the man said, "The woman whom You gave to be with me, she gave me of the tree, and I ate."

And the LORD God said to the woman, "What is this you have done?"

And the woman said, "The serpent deceived me, and I ate."

—GENESIS 3:1–18

Surely you have spoken in my hearing,
And I have heard the sound of your words,
    saying,
"I am pure, without transgression;
I am innocent, and there is no iniquity in me."
—JOB 33:8–9

Do you think this is right?
Do you say,
"My righteousness is more than God's"? . . .
Surely God will not listen to empty talk,
Nor will the Almighty regard it.
—JOB 35:2, 13

Do you see a man wise in his own eyes?
There is more hope for a fool than for him.
—PROVERBS 26:12

Woe to those who are wise in their own eyes,
And prudent in their own sight!
—ISAIAH 5:21

But we are all like an unclean thing,
And all our righteousnesses are like filthy
rags;
We all fade as a leaf,
And our iniquities, like the wind,
Have taken us away.
—ISAIAH 64:6

Jesus said to them, "If you were blind, you would have no sin; but now you say, 'We see.' Therefore your sin remains."
—JOHN 9:41

But "He who glories, let him glory in the LORD."
—2 CORINTHIANS 10:17

And He said to them, "You are those who justify yourselves before men, but God knows your hearts. For what is highly esteemed among men is an abomination in the sight of God."
—LUKE 16:15

■ *Christ, the One Who Took Our Blame*

Who has believed our report?
And to whom has the arm of the LORD been
   revealed?
For He shall grow up before Him as a tender
   plant,
And as a root out of dry ground.
He has no form or comeliness;
And when we see Him,
There is no beauty that we should desire Him.
He is despised and rejected by men,
A Man of sorrows and acquainted with grief.
And we hid, as it were, our faces from Him;
He was despised, and we did not esteem
   Him.
Surely He has borne our griefs
And carried our sorrows;
Yet we esteemed Him stricken,
Smitten by God, and afflicted.
But He was wounded for our transgressions,
He was bruised for our iniquities;
The chastisement for our peace was upon
   Him,
And by His stripes we are healed.
All we like sheep have gone astray;
We have turned, every one, to his own way;
And the LORD has laid on Him the iniquity of
   us all.
He was oppressed and He was afflicted,
Yet He opened not His mouth;

He was led as a lamb to the slaughter,
And as a sheep before its shearers is silent,
So He opened not His mouth.
He was taken from prison and from
   judgment,
And who will declare His generation?
For He was cut off from the land of the living;
For the transgressions of My people He was
   stricken.
And they made His grave with the wicked—
But with the rich at His death,
Because He had done no violence,
Nor was any deceit in His mouth.
Yet it pleased the LORD to bruise Him;
He has put Him to grief.
When You make His soul an offering for sin,
He shall see His seed, He shall prolong His
   days,
And the pleasure of the LORD shall prosper in
   His hand.
He shall see the travail of His soul, and be
   satisfied.
By His knowledge My righteous Servant shall
   justify many,
For He shall bear their iniquities.
Therefore I will divide Him a portion with the
   great,
And He shall divide the spoil with the strong,
Because He poured out His soul unto death,
And He was numbered with the
   transgressors,

And He bore the sin of many,
And made intercession for the transgressors.
—ISAIAH 53:1–12

Playing the Victim: Laborers Claim Unfairness

"For the kingdom of heaven is like a landowner who went out early in the morning to hire laborers for his vineyard. Now when he had agreed with the laborers for a denarius a day, he sent them into his vineyard.

"And he went out about the third hour and saw others standing idle in the marketplace, and said to them, 'You also go into the vineyard, and whatever is right I will give you.' And they went.

"Again he went out about the sixth and the ninth hour, and did likewise. And about the eleventh hour he went out and found others standing idle, and said to them, 'Why have you been standing here idle all day?'

"They said to him, 'Because no one hired us.'

"He said to them, 'You also go into the vineyard, and whatever is right you will receive.'

"So when evening had come, the owner of the vineyard said to his steward, 'Call the laborers and give them their wages, beginning with the last to the first.'

"And when those came who were hired about the eleventh hour, they each received a denarius. But when the first came, they supposed that they would receive more; and they likewise received each a denarius. And when they had received it, they murmured against the landowner, saying, 'These last men have worked only one hour, and you made them equal to us who have borne the burden and the heat of the day.'

"But he answered one of them and said, 'Friend, I am doing you no wrong. Did you not agree with me for a denarius? Take what is yours and go your way. I wish to give to this last man the same as to you. Is it not lawful for me to do what I wish with my own things? Or is your eye evil because I am good?'"

—MATTHEW 20:1–15

■ God, the One Who Champions Justice

The LORD is righteous
He is in her midst,
He will do no unrighteousness.
Every morning He brings His justice to light;
He never fails,
But the unjust knows no shame.
"Therefore wait for Me," says the LORD,
"Until the day I rise up for plunder;
My determination is to gather the nations
To My assembly of kingdoms,
To pour on them My indignation,
All my fierce anger;
All the earth shall be devoured
With the fire of My jealousy.

For then I will restore to the peoples a pure
	language,
That they all may call on the name of the
	LORD,
To serve Him with one accord.
From beyond the rivers of Ethiopia My
	worshipers,
The daughter of My dispersed ones,
Shall bring My offering.
In that day you shall not be shamed for any of
	your deeds
In which you transgress against Me;
For then I will take away from your midst
Those who rejoice in your pride,
And you shall no longer be haughty
In My holy mountain.
I will leave in your midst
A meek and humble people,
And they shall trust in the name of the LORD.
The remnant of Israel shall do no
	unrighteousness
And speak no lies,
Nor shall a deceitful tongue be found in their
	mouth;
For they shall feed their flocks and lie down,
And no one shall make them afraid."
Sing, O daughter of Zion!
Shout, O Israel!
Be glad and rejoice with all your heart,
O daughter of Jerusalem!
The LORD has taken away your judgments,

He has cast out your enemy.
The King of Israel, the LORD, is in your midst;
You shall see disaster no more.
In that day it shall be said to Jerusalem:
"Do not fear;
Zion, let not your hands be weak.
The LORD your God in your midst,
The Mighty One, will save;
He will rejoice over you with gladness,
He will quiet you in His love,
He will rejoice over you with singing."
I will gather those who sorrow over the
    appointed assembly,
Who are among you,
To whom its reproach is a burden.
Behold, at that time
I will deal with all who afflict you;
I will save the lame,
And gather those who were driven out;
I will appoint them for praise and fame
In every land where they were put to shame.
                            —ZEPHANIAH 3:5, 8–19

Parents: Did You Miss Out on Parental Care?

Our parents failed us! But their parents failed them, too. And our parents' parents failed, and . . . . It goes back a long way doesn't it? Ideally, a child, from day one, receives massive doses of warmth, comfort, care, and nurture, everything true parental love really ought to offer. Most of us, however, just got bits and pieces of that love—at least that's all we actually felt.

Perhaps your parents withdrew emotional support when you really needed it. Or maybe they actually stayed away, physically, by just being too busy with work or the task of dealing with their own pain. Some parents do use every bit of their own emotional energy on themselves, to deal with the adverse effects of their addictions.

Obviously, no parent is perfect. No parent has been perfectly parented. So none of us is entitled to lay blame. Yet parental failings leave a nurture-deficit deep within us. How will we fill it? To whom can we turn for the lost care and comfort?

Suggestion: Try reparenting. The Scriptures tell us that God is a Heavenly Parent, offering unconditional love, care, closeness. Of course, much of what God does for us comes by way of other human beings who have been so filled with His love that they can extend it graciously to others. But the first step for those in recovery is to find out about this Heavenly Parent and be inspired by the possibilities of a new source of care for their inner child.

Did Your Parents Fail to Meet Their Responsibilities?

■ To View Their Children as Blessings from God

At that time the disciples came to Jesus, saying, "Who then is greatest in the kingdom of heaven?"

And Jesus called a little child to Him, set him in the midst of them, and said, "Assuredly, I say to you, unless you are converted and become as little children, you will by no means enter the kingdom of heaven. Therefore whoever humbles himself as this little child is the greatest in the kingdom of heaven. And whoever receives one little child like this in My name receives Me. But whoever causes one of these little ones who believe in Me to sin, it would be better for him if a millstone were hung around his neck, and he were drowned in the depth of the sea. Woe to the world because of offenses! For offenses must come, but woe to that man by whom the offense comes! . . .

"Take heed that you do not despise one of these little ones, for I say to you that in heaven their angels always see the face of My Father who is in heaven. For the Son of Man has come to save that which was lost. What do you think? If a man has a hundred sheep, and one of them goes astray, does he not leave the ninety-nine and go to the mountains to seek the one that is straying? And if he should find it, assuredly, I say to you, he rejoices more over that sheep than over the ninety-nine that did not go astray. Even so it is not the will of your Father who is in heaven that one of these little ones should perish."

—MATTHEW 18:1-7, 10-14

■ *To Give Religious Instruction*

For I have known him, in order that he may command his children and his household after him, that they keep the way of the LORD, to do righteousness and justice.

—GENESIS 18:19

And you shall tell your son in that day, saying, "This is done because of what the LORD did for me when I came up from Egypt."

—EXODUS 13:8

Only take heed to yourself, and diligently keep yourself, lest you forget the things your eyes have seen, and lest they depart from your heart all the days of your life. And teach them to your children and your grandchildren, especially concerning the day you stood before the LORD your God in Horeb, when the LORD said to me, "Gather the people to Me, and I will let them hear My words, that they may learn to fear Me all the days they live on the earth, and that they may teach their children."

—DEUTERONOMY 4:9–10

"You shall teach them to your children, speaking of them when you sit in your house, when you walk by the way, when you lie down, and when you rise up."

—DEUTERONOMY 11:19

Train up a child in the way he should go,
And when he is old he will not depart from it.

—PROVERBS 22:6

Correct your son, and he will give you rest;
Yes, he will give delight to your soul.

—PROVERBS 29:17

Give ear, O my people, to my law;
Incline your ears to the words of my mouth.
I will open my mouth in a parable;
I will utter dark sayings of old,
Which we have heard and known,
And our fathers have told us.

We will not hide them from their children,
Telling to the generation to come the praises of
  the LORD,
And His strength and His wonderful works
  that He has done.
For He established a testimony in Jacob,
And appointed a law in Israel,
Which He commanded our fathers,
That they should make them known to their
  children;
That the generation to come might know
  them,
The children who would be born,
That they may arise and declare them to their
  children,
That they may set their hope in God,
And not forget the works of God,
But keep His commandments;
And may not be like their fathers,
A stubborn and rebellious generation,
A generation that did not set its heart aright,
And whose spirit was not faithful to God.
                                          —PSALMS 78:1–8

And these words which I command you today
shall be in your heart; you shall teach them diligently to your children, and shall talk of them
when you sit in your house, when you walk by the
way, when you lie down, and when you rise up.
You shall bind them as a sign on your hand, and
they shall be as frontlets between your eyes. You

shall write them on the doorposts of your house and on your gates.

—DEUTERONOMY 6:6–9

And you, fathers, do not provoke your children to wrath, but bring them up in the training and admonition of the Lord.

—EPHESIANS 6:4

■ *To Maintain a Loving Marriage*

[Give] thanks always for all things to God the Father in the name of our Lord Jesus Christ, submitting to one another in the fear of God.

Wives, submit to your own husbands, as to the Lord. For the husband is head of the wife, as also Christ is head of the church; and He is the Savior of the body. Therefore, just as the church is subject to Christ, so let the wives be to their own husbands in everything.

Husbands, love your wives, just as Christ also loved the church and gave Himself for it, that He might sanctify and cleanse it with the washing of water by the word, that He might present it to Himself a glorious church, not having spot or wrinkle or any such thing, but that it should be holy and without blemish.

So husbands ought to love their own wives as their own bodies; he who loves his wife loves himself. For no one ever hated his own flesh, but nourishes and cherishes it, just as the Lord does the church. For we are members of His body, of His flesh and of His bones. "For this reason a man shall leave his father and mother and be joined to his wife, and the two shall become one flesh." This is a great mystery, but I speak concerning Christ and the church.

Nevertheless let each one of you in particular so love his own wife as himself, and let the wife see that she respects her husband.

—EPHESIANS 5:21–33

■ To Be There, Not Absent

You shall not afflict any widow or fatherless child. If you afflict them in any way, and they cry at all to Me, I will surely hear their cry.

—EXODUS 22:22–23

Arise, O LORD! O God, lift up Your hand!
Do not forget the humble.
Why do the wicked renounce God?
He has said in his heart,
"You will not require an account."
But You have seen it, for You observe trouble
    and grief,
To repay it by Your hand.
The helpless commits himself to You;
You are the helper of the fatherless.
Break the arm of the wicked and the evil man;
Seek out his wickedness until You find none.
The LORD is King forever and ever;
The nations have perished out of His land.

LORD, You have heard the desire of the
    humble;
You will prepare their heart;
You will cause Your ear to hear,
To do justice to the fatherless and the
    oppressed,
That the man of the earth may oppress no
    more.

—PSALM 10:12–18

■ *To Be a Good Influence, Not Overindulgent*

Then a man of God came to Eli and said to him,
"Thus says the LORD: 'Did I not clearly reveal Myself to the house of your father when they were in
Egypt in Pharaoh's house? Did I not choose him
out of all the tribes of Israel to be My priest, to
offer upon My altar, to burn incense, and to wear
an ephod before Me? And did I not give to the
house of your father all the offerings of the children of Israel made by fire? Why do you kick at My
sacrifice and My offering which I have commanded in My habitation, and honor your sons
more than Me, to make yourselves fat with the
best of all the offerings of Israel My people?'

"Therefore the LORD God of Israel says: 'I said
indeed that your house and the house of your
father would walk before Me forever'; but now the
LORD says: 'Far be it from Me; for those who honor
Me I will honor, and those who despise Me shall
be lightly esteemed.

'Behold, the days are coming that I will cut off

your arm and the arm of your father's house, so that there will not be an old man in your house. And you will see an enemy in My habitation, despite all the good which God does for Israel. And there shall not be an old man in your house forever. But any of your men whom I do not cut off from My altar shall consume your eyes and grieve your heart. And all the descendants of your house shall die in the flower of their age.

'Now this shall be a sign to you that will come upon your two sons, on Hophni and Phinehas: in one day they shall die, both of them.'"

—1 SAMUEL 2:27–34

Will You Look to God for Reparenting?

But now, O LORD,
You are our Father;
We are the clay, and You our potter;
And all we are the work of Your hand.

—ISAIAH 64:8

"As one whom his mother comforts,
So I will comfort you;
And you shall be comforted in Jerusalem."

—ISAIAH 66:13

A father of the fatherless, a defender of
    widows,
Is God in His holy habitation.

—PSALM 68:5

You, O LORD, are our Father;
Our Redeemer from Everlasting
   is Your name.

—ISAIAH 63:16

■ *God as Good and Loving Parent*

Are not two sparrows sold for a copper coin?
And not one of them falls to the ground apart from
your Father's will.

—MATTHEW 10:29

"I will be a Father to you,
And you shall be My sons and daughters,
Says the LORD Almighty."

—2 CORINTHIANS 6:18

Behold what manner of love the Father has be-
stowed on us, that we should be called children of
God!

—1 JOHN 3:1

"Or what man is there among you who, if his
son asks for bread, will give him a stone? Or if he
asks for a fish, will he give him a serpent? If you
then, being evil, know how to give good gifts to
your children, how much more will your Father
who is in heaven give good things to those who
ask Him!"

—MATTHEW 7:9-11

He who does not love does not know God, for
God is love. In this the love of God was mani-

fested toward us, that God has sent His only begotten Son into the world, that we might live through Him.

In this is love, not that we loved God, but that He loved us and sent His Son to be the propitiation for our sins. Beloved, if God so loved us, we also ought to love one another.

No one has seen God at any time. If we love one another, God abides in us, and His love has been perfected in us. By this we know that we abide in Him, and He in us, because He has given us of His Spirit.

And we have seen and testify that the Father has sent the Son as Savior of the world. Whoever confesses that Jesus is the Son of God, God abides in him, and he in God. And we have known and believed the love that God has for us. God is love, and he who abides in love abides in God, and God in him.

Love has been perfected among us in this: that we may have boldness in the day of judgment; because as He is, so are we in this world. There is no fear in love; but perfect love casts out fear, because fear involves torment. But he who fears has not been made perfect in love. We love Him because He first loved us.

—1 JOHN 4:8-19

■ *God as Approving and Accepting Parent*

Blessed be the God and Father of our Lord Jesus Christ, who has blessed us with every spiritual blessing in the heavenly places in Christ, just as He chose us in Him before the foundation of the world, that we should be holy and without blame before Him in love, having predestined us to adoption as sons by Jesus Christ to Himself, according to the good pleasure of His will, to the praise of the glory of His grace, by which He has made us accepted in the Beloved.

—EPHESIANS 1:3–6

But in every nation whoever fears Him and works righteousness is accepted by Him.

—ACTS 10:35

You also, as living stones, are being built up a spiritual house, a holy priesthood, to offer up spiritual sacrifices acceptable to God through Jesus Christ.

—1 PETER 2:5

But God, who is rich in mercy, because of His great love with which He loved us, even when we were dead in trespasses, made us alive together with Christ (by grace you have been saved), and raised us up together, and made us sit together in the heavenly places in Christ Jesus, that in the ages to come He might show the exceeding riches of His grace in His kindness toward us in Christ Jesus. For by grace you have been saved through faith, and that not of yourselves; it is the gift of God, not of works, lest anyone should boast.

—EPHESIANS 2:4–9

■ *God as Adopting Parent*

For as many as are led by the Spirit of God, these are sons of God. For you did not receive the spirit of bondage again to fear, but you received the Spirit of adoption by whom we cry out, "Abba, Father." The Spirit Himself bears witness with our spirit that we are children of God, and if children, then heirs—heirs of God and joint heirs with Christ, if indeed we suffer with Him, that we may also be glorified together.

For I consider that the sufferings of this present time are not worthy to be compared with the glory which shall be revealed in us. For the earnest expectation of the creation eagerly waits for the revealing of the sons of God. For the creation was subjected to futility, not willingly, but because of Him who subjected it in hope; because the creation itself also will be delivered from the bondage of corruption into the glorious liberty of the children of God. For we know that the whole creation groans and labors with birth pangs together until now.

—ROMANS 8:14–22

Even so we, when we were children, were in bondage under the elements of the world. But when the fullness of the time had come, God sent forth His Son, born of a woman, born under the law, to redeem those who were under the law, that we might receive the adoption as sons. And because you are sons, God has sent forth the Spirit of

His Son into your hearts, crying out, "Abba, Father!" Therefore you are no longer a slave but a son, and if a son, then an heir of God through Christ.

—GALATIANS 4:3–7

■ God as Protecting Parent

"Fear not, for I have redeemed you;
I have called you by your name;
You are Mine.
When you pass through the waters, I will be
  with you;
And through the rivers, they shall not
  overflow you. When you walk through the
  fire, you shall not be burned,
Nor shall the flame scorch you.
For I am the LORD your God,
The Holy One of Israel, your Savior;
I gave Egypt for your ransom,
Ethiopia and Seba in your place.
Since you were precious in My sight,
You have been honored,
And I have loved you;
Therefore I will give men for you,
And people for your life.
Fear not, for I am with you;
I will bring your descendants from the east,
And gather you from the west;
I will say to the north, 'Give them up!'
And to the south, 'Do not keep them back!'

Bring My sons from afar, And My daughters
   from the ends of the earth—
Everyone who is called by My name,
Whom I have created for My glory; I have
   formed him, yes, I have made him."
                                    —ISAIAH 43:1b-7

Do You Recognize Your Responsibilities as a Child?

My son, keep your father's command,
And do not forsake the law of your mother.
                                    —PROVERBS 6:20

My son, if your heart is wise,
My heart will rejoice—indeed, I myself;
Yes, my inmost being will rejoice
When your lips speak right things.
                                    —PROVERBS 23:15-16

The father of the righteous will greatly rejoice,
And he who begets a wise child will delight in
   him.
Let your father and your mother be glad,
And let her who bore you rejoice.
My son, give me your heart,
And let your eyes observe my ways.
                                    —PROVERBS 23: 24-26

"You know the commandments: 'Do not commit adultery,' 'Do not murder,' 'Do not steal,' 'Do not bear false witness,' 'Honor your father and your mother.'"

—LUKE 18:20

Children, obey your parents in the Lord, for this is right. "Honor your father and mother," which is the first commandment with promise: "that it may be well with you and you may live long on the earth."

—EPHESIANS 6:1–3

Abuse: Did You Suffer Emotional or Physical Wounds?

Most children suffer some form of passive abuse, the sins of omission, or emotional withdrawal, that every parent commits to some extent. But for many children of alcoholics, the withdrawal of parental care was displayed in the form of active abuse. Perhaps we got up early for school, dressed ourselves, fed ourselves, taught ourselves, comforted ourselves. Maybe we even suffered excessive corporal punishment or sexual exploitation by other family members. And though our parents should have been taking care of us, we ended up taking care of them!

The hardest thing to accept about past abuse is that each of its wounds, if they are to be truly healed, must be felt not once, but many times. We must let ourselves experience those childhood pains again, as adults. But we do it now with our eyes wide open: recognizing that none of it was our fault, calling a halt to it in our memories, denouncing it for what it was—somebody else's sin. Refusing to uncover the pain and walk through it this way only hardens it and extends its ill effects in ourselves and in our children.

That's the hard part. But there is a joyful part, too. Amazingly, going back through our pain unleashes a wonderful power that only God could place within us, because it's supernatural: We eventually find the power to forgive and to move on with our lives.

Facing the Pain of Past Abuse

■ Suffering Emotional and Physical Wounds

From the sole of the foot even to the head,
There is no soundness in it,
But wounds and bruises and putrefying sores;
They have not been closed or bound up,
Or soothed with ointment.

—ISAIAH 1:6

Woe is me for my hurt!
My wound is severe.
But I say, "Truly this is an infirmity,
And I must bear it."

—JEREMIAH 10:19

Why is my pain perpetual
And my wound incurable,
Which refuses to be healed?
Will You surely be to me like an unreliable
    stream,
As waters that fail?

—JEREMIAH 15:18

My eyes fail with tears,
My heart is troubled;
My bile is poured on the ground
Because of the destruction of the daughter of
    my people,
Because the children and the infants
Faint in the streets of the city.
They say to their mothers,
"Where is grain and wine?"
As they swoon like the wounded
In the streets of the city,
As their life is poured out
In their mothers' bosom.

—LAMENTATIONS 2:11–12

Then He began to speak to them in parables: "A man planted a vineyard and set a hedge around it, dug a place for the wine vat and built a tower. And he leased it to vinedressers and went into a far country.

"Now at vintage-time he sent a servant to the vinedressers, that he might receive some of the fruit of the vineyard from the vinedressers. And they took him and beat him and sent him away empty-handed.

"Again he sent them another servant, and at him they threw stones, wounded him in the head, and sent him away shamefully treated. And again he sent another, and him they killed; and many others, beating some and killing some.

"Therefore still having one son, his beloved, he also sent him to them last, saying, 'They will respect my son.' But those vinedressers said among themselves, 'This is the heir. Come, let us kill him, and the inheritance will be ours.' And they took him and killed him and cast him out of the vineyard.

"Therefore what will the owner of the vineyard do? He will come and destroy the vinedressers, and give the vineyard to others.

"Have you not read this Scripture:
'The stone which the builders rejected
Has become the chief cornerstone.'"

—MARK 12:1–10

■ Suffering Sexual Abuse

Now after this it was so that Absalom the son of David had a lovely sister, whose name was Tamar; and Amnon the son of David loved her. Amnon was so distressed over his sister Tamar that he became sick; for she was a virgin. And it was improper for Amnon to do anything to her. . . .

Then Amnon lay down and pretended to be ill; and when the king came to see him, Amnon said to the king, "Please let Tamar my sister come and make a couple of cakes for me in my sight, that I may eat from her hand." And David sent home to Tamar, saying, "Now go to your brother Amnon's house, and prepare food for him."

So Tamar went to her brother Amnon's house; and he was lying down. Then she took flour and kneaded it, made cakes in his sight, and baked the cakes. And she took the pan and placed them out before him, but he refused to eat.

Then Amnon said, "Have everyone go out from me." And they all went out from him. Then Amnon said to Tamar, "Bring the food into the bedroom, that I may eat from your hand." And Tamar took the cakes which she had made, and brought them to Amnon her brother in the bedroom.

Now when she had brought them to him to eat, he took hold of her and said to her, "Come, lie with me, my sister." And she answered him, "No, my brother, do not force me, for no such thing should be done in Israel. Do not do this disgraceful thing! And I, where could I take my shame? And as for you, you would be like one of the fools in Israel. Now therefore, please speak to the king; for he will not withhold me from you." However, he would not heed her voice; and being stronger than she, he forced her and lay with her. . . .

Then Tamar put ashes on her head, and tore her robe of many colors that was on her, and laid her hand on her head and went away crying bitterly.

—2 SAMUEL 13:1–2, 6–14, 19

■ Suffering Abusive Parental Rage

Saul took [David] that day, and would not let him go home to his father's house anymore. And it happened on the next day that the distressing spirit from God came upon Saul, and he prophesied inside the house. So David played music with his hand, as at other times; but there was a spear in Saul's hand. And Saul cast the spear, for he said, "I will pin David to the wall!" But David escaped his presence twice.

—1 SAMUEL 18: 2, 10–11

Then Saul's anger was aroused against Jonathan, and he said to him, "You son of a perverse, rebellious woman! Do I not know that you have chosen the son of Jesse to your own shame and to the shame of your mother's nakedness? For as long as the son of Jesse lives on the earth, you shall not be established, nor your kingdom. Now therefore, send and bring him to me, for he shall surely die."

And Jonathan answered Saul his father, and said to him, "Why should he be killed? What has he done?" Then Saul cast a spear at him to kill him, by which Jonathan knew that it was determined by his father to kill David. So Jonathan arose from the table in fierce anger, and ate no food the second day of the month, for he was grieved for David, because his father had treated him shamefully.

—1 SAMUEL 20: 30–34

■ Suffering Parental Lack of Control Because of Addictive Agents

Noah and His Son

Now the sons of Noah who went out of the ark were Shem, Ham, and Japheth. And Ham was the father of Canaan. These three were the sons of Noah, and from these the whole earth was populated.

And Noah began to be a farmer, and he planted a vineyard. Then he drank of the wine and was drunk, and became uncovered in his tent. And Ham, the father of Canaan, saw the nakedness of his father, and told his two brothers outside. But Shem and Japheth took a garment, laid it on both their shoulders, and went backward and covered the nakedness of their father. Their faces were turned away, and they did not see their father's nakedness.

So Noah awoke from his wine, and knew what his younger son had done to him. Then he said:

"Cursed be Canaan;
A servant of servants
He shall be to his brethren."

—GENESIS 9:18–25

Lot and His Daughters

Then Lot went up out of Zoar and dwelt in the mountains, and his two daughters were with him;

for he was afraid to dwell in Zoar. And he and his two daughters dwelt in a cave.

Now the firstborn said to the younger, "Our father is old, and there is no man on the earth to come in to us as is the custom of all the earth. Come, let us make our father drink wine, and we will lie with him, that we may preserve the lineage of our father."

So they made their father drink wine that night. And the firstborn went in and lay with her father, and he did not know when she lay down or when she arose.

It happened on the next day that the firstborn said to the younger, "Indeed I lay with my father last night; let us make him drink wine tonight also, and you go in and lie with him, that we may preserve the lineage of our father."

Then they made their father drink wine that night also. And the younger arose and lay with him, and he did not know when she lay down or when she arose. Thus both the daughters of Lot were with child by their father.

—GENESIS 19:30–36

Finding the Comfort of God

■ God's Comfort, Strength, and Help

The LORD is my rock and my fortress and my deliverer;

My God, my strength, in whom I will trust;

My shield and the horn of my salvation, my
stronghold.
I will call upon the LORD, who is worthy to be
praised;
So shall I be saved from my enemies.
The pangs of death encompassed me,
And the floods of ungodliness made me afraid.
The sorrows of Sheol surrounded me;
The snares of death confronted me.
In my distress I called upon the LORD,
And cried out to my God;
He heard my voice from His temple,
And my cry came before Him, even to His ears.
—PSALM 18:2-6

God is our refuge and strength,
A very present help in trouble.
Therefore we will not fear,
Though the earth be removed,
And though the mountains be carried into the
    midst of the sea;
Though its waters roar and be troubled,
Though the mountains shake with its
    swelling. Selah
—PSALM 46:1-3

Cast your burden on the LORD,
And He shall sustain you;
He shall never permit the righteous to be
    moved.
—PSALM 55:22

Abuse: Did You Suffer Emotional or Physical Wounds?   45

"Come to Me, all you who labor and are heavy laden, and I will give you rest. Take My yoke upon you and learn from Me, for I am gentle and lowly in heart, and you will find rest for your souls. For My yoke is easy and My burden is light."

—MATTHEW 11:28–30

"These things I have spoken to you, that in Me you may have peace. In the world you will have tribulation; but be of good cheer, I have overcome the world."

—JOHN 16:33

■ *God's Deliverance*

He shall call upon Me, and I will answer him;
I will be with him in trouble;
I will deliver him and honor him.

—PSALM 91:15

"But I will deliver you in that day," says the LORD," and you shall not be given into the hand of the men of whom you are afraid. For I will surely deliver you, and you shall not fall by the sword; but your life shall be as a prize to you, because you have put your trust in Me," says the LORD.

—JEREMIAH 39:17–18

I sought the LORD, and He heard me,
And delivered me from all my fears.

—PSALM 34:4

"The Spirit of the Lord GOD is upon Me,
Because the LORD has anointed Me
To preach good tidings to the poor;
He has sent Me to heal the brokenhearted,
To proclaim liberty to the captives,
And the opening of the prison to those who
    are bound;
To proclaim the acceptable year of the LORD,
And the day of vengeance of our God;
To comfort all who mourn,
To console those who mourn in Zion,
To give them beauty for ashes,
The oil of joy for mourning,
The garment of praise for the spirit of
    heaviness;
That they may be called trees of
    righteousness,
The planting of the LORD, that He may be
    glorified."

—ISAIAH 61:1–3

"Most assuredly, I say to you that you will weep
and lament, but the world will rejoice; and you
will be sorrowful, but your sorrow will be turned
into joy.

"A woman, when she is in labor, has sorrow because her hour has come; but as soon as she has
given birth to the child, she no longer remembers
the anguish, for joy that a human being has been
born into the world.

"Therefore you now have sorrow; but I will see

you again and your heart will rejoice, and your joy no one will take from you.

—JOHN 16:20–22

[God is the one] who delivered us from so great a death, and does deliver us; in whom we trust that He will still deliver us.

—2 CORINTHIANS 1:10

And the Lord will deliver me from every evil work and preserve me for His heavenly kingdom. To Him be glory forever and ever. Amen!

—2 TIMOTHY 4:18

■ God's Offer of Safety

But now, thus says the LORD, who created you, O Jacob, And He who formed you, O Israel:
"Fear not, for I have redeemed you; I have called you by your name;
You are Mine.
When you pass through the waters, I will be with you; And through the rivers, they shall not overflow you. When you walk through the fire, you shall not be burned,
Nor shall the flame scorch you.

—ISAIAH 43:1–2

When you lie down, you will not be afraid;
Yes, you will lie down and your sleep will be sweet.

—PROVERBS 3:24

The LORD is my light and my salvation;
Whom shall I fear?
The LORD is the strength of my life;
Of whom shall I be afraid?
When the wicked came against me
To eat up my flesh,
My enemies and foes,
They stumbled and fell.
Though an army should encamp against me,
My heart shall not fear;
Though war should rise against me,
In this I will be confident.
One thing I have desired of the LORD,
That will I seek:
That I may dwell in the house of the LORD
All the days of my life,
To behold the beauty of the LORD,
And to inquire in His temple.
For in the time of trouble
He shall hide me in His pavilion;
In the secret place of His tabernacle
He shall hide me;
He shall set me high upon a rock.

—PSALM 27:1–5

■ God's Shepherdlike Care

For thus says the Lord GOD: "Indeed I Myself will search for My sheep and seek them out. As a shepherd seeks out his flock on the day he is among his scattered sheep, so will I seek out My sheep and deliver them from all the places where they were scattered on a cloudy and dark day.

"And I will bring them out from the peoples and gather them from the countries, and will bring them to their own land; I will feed them on the mountains of Israel, in the valleys and in all the inhabited places of the country.

"I will feed them in good pasture, and their fold shall be on the high mountains of Israel. There they shall lie down in a good fold and feed in rich pasture on the mountains of Israel.

"I will feed My flock, and I will make them lie down," says the Lord GOD. "I will seek what was lost and bring back what was driven away, bind up the broken and strengthen what was sick; but I will destroy the fat and the strong, and feed them in judgment."

—EZEKIEL 34:11–16

■ God's Healing for Wounds and Hurts

Praise the LORD!
For it is good to sing praises to our God;
For it is pleasant, and praise is beautiful.
The LORD builds up Jerusalem;
He gathers together the outcasts of Israel.
He heals the brokenhearted
And binds up their wounds.

—PSALM 147:1–3

For He bruises, but He binds up;
He wounds, but His hands make whole.

—JOB 5:18

"Therefore all those who devour you shall be
  devoured;
And all your adversaries, every one of them,
  shall go into captivity;
Those who plunder you shall become plunder,
And all who prey upon you I will make a
  prey.
For I will restore health to you
And heal you of your wounds," says the
  LORD.

—JEREMIAH 30:16–17

Freeing Myself from the Past

■ Forgiving Past Abusive Relationships

For if you forgive men their trespasses, your
heavenly Father will also forgive you. But if you do
not forgive men their trespasses, neither will your
Father forgive your trespasses.

—MATTHEW 6:14–15

Then Peter came to Him and said, "Lord, how
often shall my brother sin against me, and I forgive him? Up to seven times?" Jesus said to him,
"I do not say to you, up to seven times, but up to
seventy times seven.

"Therefore the kingdom of heaven is like a certain king who wanted to settle accounts with his
servants. And when he had begun to settle accounts, one was brought to him who owed him

ten thousand talents. But as he was not able to pay, his master commanded that he be sold, with his wife and children and all that he had, and that payment be made.

"The servant therefore fell down before him, saying, 'Master, have patience with me, and I will pay you all.' Then the master of that servant was moved with compassion, released him, and forgave him the debt.

"But that servant went out and found one of his fellow servants who owed him a hundred denarii; and he laid hands on him and took him by the throat, saying, 'Pay me what you owe!' So his fellow servant fell down at his feet and begged him, saying, 'Have patience with me, and I will pay you all.' And he would not, but went and threw him into prison till he should pay the debt.

"So when his fellow servants saw what had been done, they were very grieved, and came and told their master all that had been done. Then his master, after he had called him, said to him, 'You wicked servant! I forgave you all that debt because you begged me. Should you not also have had compassion on your fellow servant, just as I had pity on you?'

"And his master was angry, and delivered him to the torturers until he should pay all that was due to him. So My heavenly Father also will do to you if each of you, from his heart, does not forgive his brother his trespasses."

—MATTHEW 18:21–35

■ *Forgiving Family Sins of the Past*

'Thus you shall say to Joseph: "I beg you, please forgive the trespass of your brothers and their sin; for they did evil to you."' Now, please, forgive the trespass of the servants of the God of your father."

And Joseph wept when they spoke to him.

Then his brothers also went and fell down before his face, and they said, "Behold, we are your servants."

Joseph said to them, "Do not be afraid, for am I in the place of God? But as for you, you meant evil against me; but God meant it for good." . . . And he comforted them and spoke kindly to them.

—GENESIS 50:17–20a, 21

Then Peter came to Him and said, "Lord, how often shall my brother sin against me, and I forgive him? Up to seven times?" Jesus said to him, "I do not say to you, up to seven times, but up to seventy times seven." . . . 'Should you not also have had compassion on your fellow servant, just as I had pity on you?'"

—MATTHEW 18:21–22, 33

■ *Forgiving Past Abuse in the Spirit of Christ*

For this is commendable, if because of conscience toward God one endures grief, suffering wrongfully. For what credit is it if, when you are beaten for your faults, you take it patiently? But when you do good and suffer for it, if you take it patiently, this is commendable before God. For to this you were called, because Christ also suffered for us, leaving us an example, that you should follow His steps:

"Who committed no sin,

Nor was deceit found in His mouth";

who, when He was reviled, did not revile in return; when He suffered, He did not threaten, but committed Himself to Him who judges righteously;

—1 PETER 2:19–23

Let this mind be in you which was also in Christ Jesus, who, being in the form of God, did not consider it robbery to be equal with God, but made Himself of no reputation, taking the form of a servant, and coming in the likeness of men. And being found in appearance as a man, He humbled Himself and became obedient to the point of death, even the death of the cross.

Therefore God also has highly exalted Him and given Him the name which is above every name, that at the name of Jesus every knee should bow, of those in heaven, and of those on earth, and of those under the earth, and that every tongue should confess that Jesus Christ is Lord, to the glory of God the Father.

Therefore, my beloved, as you have always obeyed, not as in my presence only, but now much more in my absence, work out your own salvation with fear and trembling; for it is God who works in you both to will and to do for His good pleasure.

Do all things without murmuring and disputing, that you may become blameless and harmless, children of God without fault in the midst of a crooked and perverse generation, among whom you shine as lights in the world, holding fast the word of life, so that I may rejoice in the day of Christ that I have not run in vain or labored in vain.

—PHILIPPIANS 2:5–16

THE
PRESENT

Emotions: Can You Learn to Live with Your Feelings?

Fear. Anxiety. Anger. Sadness. Are they "good" or "bad"?
Maybe they just are. One of our biggest challenges is to learn a new way to handle feelings than the one we picked up from an alcoholic parent. Our recovery approach to life requires being with our emotions rather than running from them, feeling our feelings rather than dulling them, learning from our pain rather than avoiding it. So . . .

When was the last time you had a good cry? Or a good laugh?

Feeling Abandoned by Parents and God?

My God, My God, why have You forsaken Me?
Why are You so far from helping Me,
And from the words of My groaning?

59

O My God, I cry in the daytime, but You do
not hear;
And in the night season, and am not silent.
But You are holy,
Who inhabit the praises of Israel.
Our fathers trusted in You;
They trusted, and You delivered them.
They cried to You, and were delivered;
They trusted in You, and were not ashamed.
But I am a worm, and no man;
A reproach of men, and despised of the
people.
All those who see Me laugh to scorn Me;
They shoot out the lip, they shake the head,
saying,
"He trusted in the LORD, let Him rescue Him;
Let Him deliver Him, since He delights in
Him!"
But You are He who took Me out of the
womb;
You made Me trust when I was on My
mother's breasts.
I was cast upon You from birth.
From My mother's womb
You have been My God.
Be not far from Me,
For trouble is near;
For there is none to help. . . .
But You, O LORD, do not be far from Me;
O My Strength, hasten to help Me!

—PSALM 22: 1–11, 19

. . . God Hears the Cry of the Abandoned

You who fear the LORD, praise Him!
All you descendants of Jacob, glorify Him,
And fear Him, all you offspring of Israel!
For He has not despised nor abhorred the
    affliction of the afflicted;
Nor has He hidden His face from Him;
But when He cried to Him, He heard.

—PSALM 22:23–24

Feeling Anxious and Worried?

My heart is in turmoil and cannot rest;
Days of affliction confront me.

—JOB 30:27

I am feeble and severely broken;
I groan because of the turmoil of my heart.

—PSALM 38:8

Fear came upon me, and trembling,
Which made all my bones shake.

—JOB 4:14

My heart wavered, fearfulness frightened me;
The night for which I longed He turned into
    fear for me.

—ISAIAH 21:4

. . . Give Your Worries to God

"Do not worry about your life, what you will eat or what you will drink; nor about your body, what you will put on. Is not life more than food and the body more than clothing? Look at the birds of the air, for they neither sow nor reap nor gather into barns; yet your heavenly Father feeds them. Are you not of more value than they? Which of you by worrying can add one cubit to his stature?

"So why do you worry about clothing? Consider the lilies of the field, how they grow: they neither toil nor spin; and yet I say to you that even Solomon in all his glory was not arrayed like one of these.

"Now if God so clothes the grass of the field, which today is, and tomorrow is thrown into the oven, will He not much more clothe you, O you of little faith?

"Therefore do not worry, saying, 'What shall we eat?' or 'What shall we drink?' or 'What shall we wear?' For after all these things the Gentiles seek. For your heavenly Father knows that you need all these things. But seek first the kingdom of God and His righteousness, and all these things shall be added to you.

"Therefore do not worry about tomorrow, for tomorrow will worry about its own things. Sufficient for the day is its own trouble."

—MATTHEW 6:25–34

Feeling Fearful?

For I hear the slander of many;
Fear is on every side;
While they take counsel together against me,
They scheme to take away my life.

—PSALM 31:13

"But I will show you whom you should fear:
Fear Him who, after He has killed, has power to
cast into hell; yes, I say to you, fear Him!

—LUKE 12:5

. . . Meet Fear with Divine Courage

Though an army should encamp against me,
My heart shall not fear;
Though war should rise against me,
In this I will be confident.

—PSALM 27:3

For God has not given us a spirit of fear, but of
power and of love and of a sound mind.

—2 TIMOTHY 1:7

Therefore we will not fear,
Though the earth be removed,
And though the mountains be carried into the
midst of the sea.

—PSALM 46:2

But whoever listens to me will dwell safely,
And will be secure, without fear of evil.

—PROVERBS 1:33

"Listen to Me, you who know righteousness,
You people in whose heart is My law:
Do not fear the reproach of men,
Nor be afraid of their revilings.

—ISAIAH 51:7

"Be strong and of good courage, do not fear nor be afraid of them; for the LORD your God, He is the One who goes with you. He will not leave you nor forsake you."

—DEUTERONOMY 31:6

"The very hairs of your head are all numbered. Do not fear therefore; you are of more value than many sparrows."

—LUKE 12:7

"Do not fear, little flock, for it is your Father's good pleasure to give you the kingdom."

—LUKE 12:32

There is no fear in love; but perfect love casts out fear, because fear involves torment. But he who fears has not been made perfect in love.

—1 JOHN 4:18

"Have I not commanded you? Be strong and of good courage; do not be afraid, nor be dismayed, for the LORD your God is with you wherever you go."

—JOSHUA 1:9

Holding in Anger?

Then God saw [the Ninevites'] works, that they turned from their evil way; and God relented from the disaster that He had said He would bring upon them, and He did not do it.

—JONAH 3:10

But it displeased Jonah exceedingly, and he became angry. So he prayed to the LORD. . . . "Therefore now, O LORD, please take my life from me, for it is better for me to die than to live!" Then the LORD said, "Is it right for you to be angry?"

So Jonah went out of the city and sat on the east side of the city. There he made himself a shelter and sat under it in the shade, till he might see what would become of the city.

And the LORD God prepared a plant and made it come up over Jonah, that it might be shade for his head to deliver him from his misery. So Jonah was very grateful for the plant.

But as morning dawned the next day God prepared a worm, and it so damaged the plant that it withered. And it happened, when the sun arose, that God prepared a vehement east wind; and the sun beat on Jonah's head, so that he grew faint. Then he wished death for himself, and said, "It is better for me to die than to live."

Then God said to Jonah, "Is it right for you to be angry about the plant?"

And he said, "It is right for me to be angry, even to death!"

—JONAH 4:1–2, 3–9

. . . Express Anger Properly

But the LORD said, "You have had pity on the plant for which you have not labored, nor made it grow, which came up in a night and perished in a night. And should I not pity Nineveh, that great city, in which are more than one hundred and twenty thousand persons who cannot discern between their right hand and their left—and much livestock?"

—JONAH 4:10–11

Be angry, and do not sin.
Meditate within your heart on your bed, and
  be still.

—PSALM 4:4

"But I say to you that whoever is angry with his brother without a cause shall be in danger of the judgment. And whoever says to his brother, 'Raca!' shall be in danger of the council. But whoever says, 'You fool!' shall be in danger of hell fire."

—MATTHEW 5:22

"Be angry, and do not sin": do not let the sun go down on your wrath.

—EPHESIANS 4:26

Feel Like a Failure?

My iniquities have gone over my head;
Like a heavy burden they are too heavy for
   me. . . .
I am feeble and severely broken;
I groan because of the turmoil of my heart.
Lord, all my desire is before You;
And my sighing is not hidden from You.
My heart pants, my strength fails me;
As for the light of my eyes, it also has gone
   from me. My loved ones and my friends
   stand aloof from my plague,
And my kinsmen stand afar off.

—PSALM 38:4, 8–11

. . . God Promises Success through Obedience

After the death of Moses the servant of the LORD, it came to pass that the LORD spoke to

Joshua the son of Nun, Moses' assistant, saying: "Moses My servant is dead. Now therefore, arise, go over this Jordan, you and all this people, to the land which I am giving to them—the children of Israel.

"Every place that the sole of your foot will tread upon I have given you, as I said to Moses. From the wilderness and this Lebanon as far as the great river, the River Euphrates, all the land of the Hittites, and to the Great Sea toward the going down of the sun, shall be your territory.

"No man shall be able to stand before you all the days of your life; as I was with Moses, so I will be with you. I will not leave you nor forsake you.

"Be strong and of good courage, for to this people you shall divide as an inheritance the land which I swore to their fathers to give them. Only be strong and very courageous, that you may observe to do according to all the law which Moses My servant commanded you; do not turn from it to the right hand or to the left, that you may prosper wherever you go. This Book of the Law shall not depart from your mouth, but you shall meditate in it day and night, that you may observe to do according to all that is written in it. For then you will make your way prosperous, and then you will have good success."

—JOSHUA 1:1–8

Having Feelings of Despair?

Then Satan went out from the presence of the LORD, and struck Job with painful boils from the sole of his foot to the crown of his head. And he took for himself a potsherd with which to scrape himself while he sat in the midst of the ashes. Then his wife said to him, "Do you still hold to your integrity? Curse God and die!"

—JOB 2:7–9

. . . God Saves Us from Despair

But he said to her, "You speak as one of the foolish women speaks. Shall we indeed accept good from God, and shall we not accept adversity?" In all this Job did not sin with his lips.

—JOB 2:10

I will extol You, O LORD, for You have lifted
    me up,
And have not let my foes rejoice over me.
O LORD my God, I cried out to You,
And You have healed me.
O LORD, You have brought my soul up from
    the grave;
You have kept me alive, that I should not go
    down to the pit.
Sing praise to the LORD, You saints of His,

And give thanks at the remembrance of His
   holy name.
For His anger is but for a moment, His favor is
   for life;
Weeping may endure for a night,
But joy comes in the morning.

—PSALM 30:1–5

Feeling Ashamed?

My dishonor is continually before me,
And the shame of my face has covered me.

—PSALM 44:15

You know my reproach, my shame, and my
   dishonor;
My adversaries are all before You.

—PSALM 69:19

. . . God Replaces Shame with Joy

In You, O Lord, I put my trust;
Let me never be put to shame.

—PSALM 71:1

"Do not fear, for you will not be ashamed;
Nor be disgraced, for you will not be put to
   shame;
For you will forget the shame of your youth."

—ISAIAH 54:4

Instead of your shame you shall have double
  honor,
And instead of confusion they shall rejoice in
  their portion.
Therefore in their land they shall possess
  double;
Everlasting joy shall be theirs.

—ISAIAH 61:7

You shall eat in plenty and be satisfied,
And praise the name of the LORD your God,
Who has dealt wondrously with you;
And My people shall never be put to shame.
Then you shall know that I am in the midst of
  Israel,
And that I am the LORD your God
And there is no other.
My people shall never be put to shame.

—JOEL 2:26–27

As it is written:

"Behold, I lay in Zion a stumbling stone and
  rock of offense,
And whoever believes on Him will not be put
  to shame."

—ROMANS 9:33

Looking unto Jesus, the author and finisher of
our faith, who for the joy that was set before Him

endured the cross, despising the shame, and has
sat down at the right hand of the throne of God.
—HEBREWS 12:2

Experiencing Grief?

"Oh, that my grief were fully weighed,
And my calamity laid with it in the balances!"
—JOB 6:2

"Though I speak, my grief is not relieved;
And though I remain silent, how am I eased?"
—JOB 16:6

My eye wastes away because of grief;
It grows old because of all my enemies.
—PSALM 6:7

He is despised and rejected by men,
A Man of sorrows and acquainted with grief.
And we hid, as it were, our faces from Him;
He was despised, and we did not esteem
  Him.
Surely He has borne our griefs
And carried our sorrows;
Yet we esteemed Him stricken,
Smitten by God, and afflicted. . . .
Yet it pleased the LORD to bruise Him;
He has put Him to grief.
When You make His soul an offering for sin,

He shall see His seed, He shall prolong His
  days,
And the pleasure of the LORD shall prosper in
  His hand.

—ISAIAH 53:3-4, 10

For this is commendable, if because of conscience toward God one endures grief, suffering
wrongfully.

—1 PETER 2:19

. . . Seek God's Comfort in Grief

But You have seen it, for You observe trouble
  and grief,
To repay it by Your hand.
The helpless commits himself to You;
You are the helper of the fatherless.

—PSALM 10:14

Though He causes grief,
Yet He will show compassion
According to the multitude of His mercies.

—LAMENTATIONS 3:32

In this you greatly rejoice, though now for a little while, if need be, you have been grieved by var-
ious trials.

—1 PETER 1:6

. . . And Remember: God Promises an End to Sorrow and Death

For I delivered to you first of all that which I also received: that Christ died for our sins according to the Scriptures, and that He was buried, and that He rose again the third day according to the Scriptures. . . .

Now if Christ is preached that He has been raised from the dead, how do some among you say that there is no resurrection of the dead? But if there is no resurrection of the dead, then Christ is not risen. And if Christ is not risen, then our preaching is vain and your faith is also vain.

Yes, and we are found false witnesses of God, because we have testified of God that He raised up Christ, whom He did not raise up—if in fact the dead do not rise. For if the dead do not rise, then Christ is not risen. And if Christ is not risen, your faith is futile; you are still in your sins! Then also those who have fallen asleep in Christ have perished.

If in this life only we have hope in Christ, we are of all men the most pitiable. But now Christ is risen from the dead, and has become the firstfruits of those who have fallen asleep. . . .

Behold, I tell you a mystery: We shall not all sleep, but we shall all be changed—in a moment, in the twinkling of an eye, at the last trumpet. For the trumpet will sound, and the dead will be raised incorruptible, and we shall be changed.

For this corruptible must put on incorruption, and this mortal must put on immortality. So when this corruptible has put on incorruption, and this mortal has put on immortality, then shall be brought to pass the saying that is written: "Death is swallowed up in victory."

"O Death, where is your sting?
O Hades, where is your victory?"
—1 CORINTHIANS 15:3–4, 12–20, 51–55

After these things I looked, and behold, a great multitude which no one could number, of all nations, tribes, peoples, and tongues, standing before the throne and before the Lamb, clothed with white robes, with palm branches in their hands, and crying out with a loud voice, saying, "Salvation belongs to our God who sits on the throne, and to the Lamb!" And all the angels stood around the throne and the elders and the four living creatures, and fell on their faces before the throne and worshiped God, saying:

"Amen! Blessing and glory and wisdom,
Thanksgiving and honor and power and
   might,
Be to our God forever and ever. Amen."

Then one of the elders answered, saying to me, "Who are these arrayed in white robes, and where did they come from?"

And I said to him, "Sir, you know."

So he said to me, "These are the ones who come out of the great tribulation, and washed their robes and made them white in the blood of the Lamb. Therefore they are before the throne of God, and serve Him day and night in His temple. And He who sits on the throne will dwell among them. They shall neither hunger anymore nor thirst anymore; the sun shall not strike them, nor any heat; for the Lamb who is in the midst of the throne will shepherd them and lead them to living fountains of waters. And God will wipe away every tear from their eyes."

—REVELATION 7:9–17

CHAPTER 5

Self-Esteem: Can You Change Your Self-Image?

Imagine sitting across from yourself in a roomful of people, say, at a party. What do you see? How does that person act? What is that person likely thinking about the others in the room, and about himself or herself? Do you think you would like that person? Could you become that person's friend?

It's tough to get to be good friends with ourselves when raised in a dysfunctional and/or abusive family of origin. We got the message that we were in the way. We were a bother to those who had more important things to do than to watch out for us. We may have been an "accident" that never should have happened. So it went . . . with the result that we grew up being significantly down on ourselves. Actually, we've probably been quite unfriendly, for a long time, to the "me" who longs for love and acceptance.

The Bible calls us to change our negative

self-perceptions to be more in line with the way things really are, i.e., the way God sees them. As the old preacher used to say: "And if God sees it that way, then how is it?" In this approach to life we see the possibility of tremendous change, the potential ability to really like ourselves. That's possible because of the amazing insight that comes to people who read Scripture promises like the ones below: God not only loves me; God likes me, too!

Seeing My True Worth

■ *I Was Created by the Creator*

Then God said, "Let Us make man in Our image, according to Our likeness; let them have dominion over the fish of the sea, over the birds of the air, and over the cattle, over all the earth and over every creeping thing that creeps on the earth." So God created man in His own image; in the image of God He created him; male and female He created them. Then God blessed them, and God said to them, "Be fruitful and multiply; fill the earth and subdue it; have dominion over the fish of the sea, over the birds of the air, and over every living thing that moves on the earth." And God said, "See, I have given you every herb that yields seed which is on the face of all the earth, and every tree whose fruit yields seed; to you it shall be for food. Also, to every beast of the earth, to every bird of the air, and to everything that creeps on the earth, in which there is life, I have given every green herb for food"; and it was so. Then God saw everything that He had made, and indeed it was very good.

—GENESIS 1:27–31

■ *I Was Born for a Purpose: To Do God's Will*

Do not love the world or the things in the world. If anyone loves the world, the love of the Father is not in him. For all that is in the world—the lust of the flesh, the lust of the eyes, and the pride of life—is not of the Father but is of the world. And the world is passing away, and the lust of it; but he who does the will of God abides forever.

—1 JOHN 2:15–17

For whatever is born of God overcomes the world. And this is the victory that has overcome the world—our faith. Who is he who overcomes the world, but he who believes that Jesus is the Son of God?

—1 JOHN 5:4–5

■ *I Have a Position of Honor in the Cosmos*

O LORD, our Lord,
How excellent is Your name in all the earth,
You who set Your glory above the heavens!
Out of the mouth of babes and infants

You have ordained strength,
Because of Your enemies,
That You may silence the enemy and the
   avenger.
When I consider Your heavens, the work of
   Your fingers,
The moon and the stars, which You have
   ordained,
What is man that You are mindful of him,
And the son of man that You visit him?
For You have made him a little lower than the
   angels,
And You have crowned him with glory and
   honor.
You have made him to have dominion over the
   works of Your hands;
You have put all things under his feet,
All sheep and oxen—
Even the beasts of the field,
The birds of the air,
And the fish of the sea
That pass through the paths of the seas.
O LORD, our Lord,
How excellent is Your name in all the earth!
                                —PSALM 8:1–9

■ *I Am Sustained by God's Words*

Then Jesus was led up by the Spirit into the
wilderness to be tempted by the devil. And when
He had fasted forty days and forty nights, afterward He was hungry. Now when the tempter

came to Him, he said, "If You are the Son of God, command that these stones become bread." But He answered and said, "It is written, 'Man shall not live by bread alone, but by every word that proceeds from the mouth of God.'" . . . Again, the devil took Him up on an exceedingly high mountain, and showed Him all the kingdoms of the world and their glory. And he said to Him, "All these things I will give You if You will fall down and worship me." Then Jesus said to him, "Away with you, Satan! For it is written, 'You shall worship the LORD your God, and Him only you shall serve.'" Then the devil left Him, and behold, angels came and ministered to Him.

—MATTHEW 4:1–4, 8–11

■ *I Have Goals and Priorities of Eternal Significance*

"For what is a man profited if he gains the whole world, and loses his own soul? Or what will a man give in exchange for his soul?"

—MATTHEW 16:26

"He who loves his life will lose it, and he who hates his life in this world will keep it for eternal life."

—JOHN 12:25

Therefore, if you died with Christ from the basic principles of the world, why, as though living in the world, do you subject yourselves to regulations?

—COLOSSIANS 2:20

But God forbid that I should glory except in the cross of our Lord Jesus Christ, by whom the world has been crucified to me, and I to the world.

—GALATIANS 6:14

Then the seventh angel sounded: And there were loud voices in heaven, saying, "The kingdoms of this world have become the kingdoms of our Lord and of His Christ, and He shall reign forever and ever!"

—REVELATION 11:15

Seeing Myself through God's Eyes

■ God Sees the Potential in Me

Moses Shows Low Self-Esteem . . .

Now Moses kept the flock of Jethro his father-in-law, the priest of Midian. And he led the flock to the back of the desert, and came to Horeb, the mountain of God.

And the Angel of the LORD appeared to him in a flame of fire from the midst of a bush. So he looked, and behold, the bush burned with fire, but the bush was not consumed. Then Moses said, "I will now turn aside and see this great sight, why the bush does not burn."

So when the LORD saw that he turned aside to look, God called to him from the midst of the bush and said, "Moses, Moses!"

And he said, "Here I am."

Then He said, "Do not draw near this place. Take your sandals off your feet, for the place where you stand is holy ground." Moreover He said, "I am the God of your father—the God of Abraham, the God of Isaac, and the God of Jacob."

And Moses hid his face, for he was afraid to look upon God. . . .

"Come now, therefore, and I will send you to Pharaoh that you may bring My people, the children of Israel, out of Egypt." But Moses said to God, "Who am I?"

—EXODUS 3:1-6, 10-11

. . . But God Knew How His Epitaph Would Read!

There has not arisen in Israel a prophet like Moses, whom the LORD knew face to face, in all the signs and wonders which the LORD sent him to do in the land of Egypt, before Pharaoh, before all his servants, and in all his land, and by all that mighty power and all the great terror which Moses performed in the sight of all Israel.

—DEUTERONOMY 34:10-12

■ *God Sees Me as a Treasure . . .*

"Then the righteous will shine forth as the sun in the kingdom of their Father. He who has ears to hear, let him hear!

"Again, the kingdom of heaven is like treasure hidden in a field, which a man found and hid; and for joy over it he goes and sells all that he has and buys that field."

—MATTHEW 13:43–44

■ *. . . And as a Pearl . . .*

"Again, the kingdom of heaven is like a merchant seeking beautiful pearls, who, when he had found one pearl of great price, went and sold all that he had and bought it."

—MATTHEW 13:45–46

■ *. . . And as a Great Catch!*

"Again, the kingdom of heaven is like a dragnet that was cast into the sea and gathered some of every kind, which, when it was full, they drew to shore; and they sat down and gathered the good into vessels, but threw the bad away. So it will be at the end of the age. The angels will come forth, separate the wicked from among the just."

—MATTHEW 13:47–49

■ *God Is on My Side*

What then shall we say to these things? If God is for us, who can be against us? He who did not spare His own Son, but delivered Him up for us all, how shall He not with Him also freely give us all things?

Who shall bring a charge against God's elect? It is God who justifies. Who is he who condemns?

It is Christ who died, and furthermore is also risen, who is even at the right hand of God, who also makes intercession for us. Who shall separate us from the love of Christ? Shall tribulation, or distress, or persecution, or famine, or nakedness, or peril, or sword? As it is written:

"For Your sake we are killed all day long;
We are accounted as sheep for the slaughter."

Yet in all these things we are more than conquerors through Him who loved us. For I am persuaded that neither death nor life, nor angels nor principalities nor powers, nor things present nor things to come, nor height nor depth, nor any other created thing, shall be able to separate us from the love of God which is in Christ Jesus our Lord.

—ROMANS 8:31–39

■ *God Calls Me Away from Self-Shaming Thoughts*

Do not fear, for you will not be ashamed;
Nor be disgraced, for you will not be put to
  shame;
For you will forget the shame of your youth.
—ISAIAH 54:4

Instead of your shame you shall have double
  honor,
And instead of confusion they shall rejoice in
  their portion.
Therefore in their land they shall possess
  double;
Everlasting joy shall be theirs.
—ISAIAH 61:7

You shall eat in plenty and be satisfied,
And praise the name of the LORD your God,
Who has dealt wondrously with you;
And My people shall never be put to shame.
Then you shall know that I am in the midst of
  Israel,
And that I am the LORD your God
And there is no other.
My people shall never be put to shame.
—JOEL 2:26–27

I sought the LORD, and He heard me,
And delivered me from all my fears.

They looked to Him and were radiant,
And their faces were not ashamed.

—PSALM 34:4–5

As it is written:

"Behold, I lay in Zion a stumbling stone and
  rock of offense,
And whoever believes on Him will not be put
  to shame."

—ROMANS 9:33

■ *God Promises to Guide Me through Life*

I will instruct you and teach you in the way
  you should go;
I will guide you with My eye.

—PSALM 32:1, 6–8

Trust in the LORD with all your heart,
And lean not on your own understanding;
In all your ways acknowledge Him,
And He shall direct your paths.

—PROVERBS 3:5–6

Seeing My Life through Good Self-Esteem

■ *I Will Guard Against Self-Pity*

And Job spoke, and said:

"May the day perish on which I was born,
And the night in which it was said,
'A male child is conceived.'
May that day be darkness;
May God above not seek it,
Nor the light shine upon it.
May darkness and the shadow of death claim
    it;
May a cloud settle on it;
May the blackness of the day terrify it.
As for that night, may darkness seize it;
May it not be included among the days of the
    year,
May it not come into the number of the
    months.
Oh, may that night be barren!
May no joyful shout come into it!
May those curse it who curse the day,
Those who are ready to arouse Leviathan.
May the stars of its morning be dark;
May it look for light, but have none,
And not see the dawning of the day;
Because it did not shut up the doors of my
    mother's womb,
Nor hide sorrow from my eyes.
Why did I not die at birth?
Why did I not perish when I came from the
    womb?
Why did the knees receive me?
Or why the breasts, that I should nurse?
For now I would have lain still and been
    quiet,

I would have been asleep;
Then I would have been at rest."

—JOB 3:2-13

■ *I Will Not Expect Unconditional Approval from Others*

"If the world hates you, you know that it hated Me before it hated you.

"If you were of the world, the world would love its own. Yet because you are not of the world, but I chose you out of the world, therefore the world hates you.

"Remember the word that I said to you, 'A servant is not greater than his master.' If they persecuted Me, they will also persecute you. If they kept My word, they will keep yours also. But all these things they will do to you for My name's sake, because they do not know Him who sent Me.

"If I had not come and spoken to them, they would have no sin, but now they have no excuse for their sin.

"He who hates Me hates My Father also.

"If I had not done among them the works which no one else did, they would have no sin; but now they have seen and also hated both Me and My Father.

"But this happened that the word might be fulfilled which is written in their law, 'They hated Me without a cause.'"

—JOHN 15:18-25

■ I Will Not Expect to Escape Troubles Just Because I Believe

Beloved, do not think it strange concerning the fiery trial which is to try you, as though some strange thing happened to you; but rejoice to the extent that you partake of Christ's sufferings, that when His glory is revealed, you may also be glad with exceeding joy. If you are reproached for the name of Christ, blessed are you, for the Spirit of glory and of God rests upon you. On their part He is blasphemed, but on your part He is glorified.

But let none of you suffer as a murderer, a thief, an evildoer, or as a busybody in other people's matters. Yet if anyone suffers as a Christian, let him not be ashamed, but let him glorify God in this matter.

For the time has come for judgment to begin at the house of God; and if it begins with us first, what will be the end of those who do not obey the gospel of God? Now

"If the righteous one is scarcely saved,

Where will the ungodly and the sinner appear?"

Therefore let those who suffer according to the will of God commit their souls to Him in doing good, as to a faithful Creator.

—1 PETER 4:12–19

Blessed are you when they revile and persecute you, and say all kinds of evil against you falsely for My sake. Rejoice and be exceedingly glad, for great is your reward in heaven, for so they persecuted the prophets who were before you.

—MATTHEW 5:11–12

CHAPTER 6

Accountability: Can You Uphold Your New Responsibilities?

Reality check: I still contribute to my pain. What occurred in the past, when I was a child, was mostly not my fault. Things happened to me. Things were done to me. Most of those events were beyond my control, and I'm dealing with the pain of that fact. But I must face my daily choices in the present too. Here's where I do have some control.

Perhaps many past decisions have have been poor ones. So I look at alternatives for future decisions and determine to make better choices. Though the past is no longer in my control, I'm responsible for how things go from now on.

Biblical accountability calls me to recognize and admit my personal shortcomings to myself and to caring others. As I humbly ask for forgiveness and the removal of shortcomings in my life, I launch into a continual process of confronting rather than denying the true nature of my life—an ongoing reality check.

The Requirements

■ *Revealed: Every Act!*

In the meantime, when an innumerable multitude of people had gathered together, so that they trampled one another, He began to say to His disciples first of all, "Beware of the leaven of the Pharisees, which is hypocrisy. For there is nothing covered that will not be revealed, nor hidden that will not be known. Therefore whatever you have spoken in the dark will be heard in the light, and what you have spoken in the ear in inner rooms will be proclaimed on the housetops.

"And I say to you, My friends, do not be afraid of those who kill the body, and after that have no more that they can do. But I will show you whom you should fear: Fear Him who, after He has killed, has power to cast into hell; yes, I say to you, fear Him!"

—LUKE 12:1–5

For the word of God is living and powerful, and sharper than any two-edged sword, piercing even to the division of soul and spirit, and of joints and marrow, and is a discerner of the thoughts and intents of the heart. And there is no creature hidden from His sight, but all things are naked and open to the eyes of Him to whom we must give account.

Seeing then that we have a great High Priest who has passed through the heavens, Jesus the Son of God, let us hold fast our confession. For we do not have a High Priest who cannot sympathize with our weaknesses, but was in all points tempted as we are, yet without sin.

Let us therefore come boldly to the throne of grace, that we may obtain mercy and find grace to help in time of need.

—HEBREWS 4:12–16

■ Recognize: The True Nature of Sin

Now the works of the flesh are evident, which are: adultery, fornication, uncleanness, licentiousness, idolatry, sorcery, hatred, contentions, jealousies, outbursts of wrath, selfish ambitions, dissensions, heresies, envy, murders, drunkenness, revelries, and the like; of which I tell you beforehand, just as I also told you in time past, that those who practice such things will not inherit the kingdom of God.

—GALATIANS 5:19–21

But fornication and all uncleanness or covetousness, let it not even be named among you, as is fitting for saints; neither filthiness, nor foolish talking, nor coarse jesting, which are not fitting, but rather giving of thanks. For this you know, that no fornicator, unclean person, nor covetous man, who is an idolater, has any inheritance in the kingdom of Christ and God. Let no one deceive you with empty words, for because of these things the wrath of God comes upon the sons of disobedience. Therefore do not be partakers with them.

—EPHESIANS 5:3–7

Whoever commits sin also commits lawlessness, and sin is lawlessness. And you know that He was manifested to take away our sins, and in Him there is no sin. Whoever abides in Him does not sin. Whoever sins has neither seen Him nor known Him. Little children, let no one deceive you. He who practices righteousness is righteous, just as He is righteous. He who sins is of the devil, for the devil has sinned from the beginning. For this purpose the Son of God was manifested, that He might destroy the works of the devil. Whoever has been born of God does not sin, for His seed remains in him; and he cannot sin, because he has been born of God.

—1 JOHN 3:4–9

■ Right Living: A Matter of the Heart, Not of Rules

"Woe to you, scribes and Pharisees, hypocrites! For you pay tithe of mint and anise and cumin, and have neglected the weightier matters of the law: justice and mercy and faith. These you ought to have done, without leaving the others undone. Blind guides, who strain out a gnat and swallow a camel!

"Woe to you, scribes and Pharisees, hypocrites! For you cleanse the outside of the cup and dish, but inside they are full of extortion and self-indulgence.

"Blind Pharisee, first cleanse the inside of the cup and dish, that the outside of them may be clean also.

"Woe to you, scribes and Pharisees, hypocrites! For you are like whitewashed tombs which indeed appear beautiful outwardly, but inside are full of dead men's bones and all uncleanness. Even so you also outwardly appear righteous to men, but inside you are full of hypocrisy and lawlessness."

—MATTHEW 23:23–28

"No one, when he has lit a lamp, puts it in a secret place or under a basket, but on a lampstand, that those who come in may see the light.

"The lamp of the body is the eye. Therefore, when your eye is good, your whole body also is full of light. But when your eye is bad, your body also is full of darkness.

"Therefore take heed that the light which is in you is not darkness.

"If then your whole body is full of light, having no part dark, the whole body will be full of light, as when the bright shining of a lamp gives you light."

—LUKE 11:33–36

Also He spoke this parable to some who trusted in themselves that they were righteous, and despised others:

"Two men went up to the temple to pray, one a Pharisee and the other a tax collector. The Pharisee stood and prayed thus with himself, 'God, I thank You that I am not like other men—extortioners, unjust, adulterers, or even as this tax collector. I fast twice a week; I give tithes of all that I possess.'

"And the tax collector, standing afar off, would not so much as raise his eyes to heaven, but beat his breast, saying, 'God, be merciful to me a sinner!'

"I tell you, this man went down to his house justified rather than the other; for everyone who exalts himself will be abased, and he who humbles himself will be exalted."

—LUKE 18:9–14

■ Real Fulfillment of the Law: 'Love Your Neighbor'

For if there should come into your assembly a man with gold rings, in fine apparel, and there should also come in a poor man in filthy clothes, and you pay attention to the one wearing the fine clothes and say to him, "You sit here in a good place," and say to the poor man, "You stand there," or, "Sit here at my footstool," have you not shown partiality among yourselves, and become judges with evil thoughts? Listen, my beloved brethren: Has God not chosen the poor of this world to be rich in faith and heirs of the kingdom which He promised to those who love Him? But you have dishonored the poor man.

Do not the rich oppress you and drag you into the courts? Do they not blaspheme that noble name by which you are called? If you really fulfill the royal law according to the Scripture, "You shall love your neighbor as yourself," you do well.

—JAMES 2:2-8

My Responsibilities

■ Adjust Life-style To Keep from Sin

"You have heard that it was said to those of old, 'You shall not commit adultery.' But I say to you that whoever looks at a woman to lust for her has already committed adultery with her in his heart.

"And if your right eye causes you to sin, pluck it out and cast it from you; for it is more profitable for you that one of your members perish, than for your whole body to be cast into hell.

"And if your right hand causes you to sin, cut it off and cast it from you; for it is more profitable for you that one of your members perish, than for your whole body to be cast into hell."

—MATTHEW 5:27-30

And do this, knowing the time, that now it is high time to awake out of sleep; for now our salvation is nearer than when we first believed. The night is far spent, the day is at hand. Therefore let us cast off the works of darkness, and let us put on the armor of light. Let us walk properly, as in the day, not in revelry and drunkenness, not in licentiousness and lewdness, not in strife and envy. But put on the Lord Jesus Christ, and make no provision for the flesh, to fulfill its lusts.

—ROMANS 13:11–14

■ Accept Correction

And you have forgotten the exhortation which speaks to you as to sons:

"My son, do not despise the chastening of the LORD,
Nor be discouraged when you are rebuked by Him;
For whom the LORD loves He chastens,
And scourges every son whom He receives."

If you endure chastening, God deals with you as with sons; for what son is there whom a father does not chasten? But if you are without chastening, of which all have become partakers, then you are illegitimate and not sons.

Furthermore, we have had human fathers who corrected us, and we paid them respect. Shall we not much more readily be in subjection to the Father of spirits and live? For they indeed for a few days chastened us as seemed best to them, but He for our profit, that we may be partakers of His holiness. Now no chastening seems to be joyful for the present, but grievous; nevertheless, afterward it yields the peaceable fruit of righteousness to those who have been trained by it.

—HEBREWS 12:5–11

Good and upright is the LORD;
Therefore He teaches sinners in the way.
The humble He guides in justice,
And the humble He teaches His way.
All the paths of the LORD are mercy and truth,
    To such as keep His covenant and His
    testimonies.
For Your name's sake, O LORD,
Pardon my iniquity, for it is great.

—PSALM 25:8–11

■ Avoid Alcohol Temptation

Who has woe?
Who has sorrow?
Who has contentions?
Who has complaints?
Who has wounds without cause?
Who has redness of eyes?
Those who linger long at the wine,
Those who go in search of mixed wine.
Do not look on the wine when it is red,
When it sparkles in the cup,
When it swirls around smoothly;
At the last it bites like a serpent,
And stings like a viper.

Your eyes will see strange things,
And your heart will utter perverse things.
Yes, you will be like one who lies down in the
  midst of the sea,
Or like one who lies at the top of the mast,
  saying:
"They have struck me, but I was not hurt;
They have beaten me, but I did not feel it.
When shall I awake, that I may seek another
  drink?"

—PROVERBS 23:29–35

■ *Avoid Sexual Temptation*

My son, pay attention to my wisdom;
Lend your ear to my understanding,
That you may preserve discretion,
And your lips may keep knowledge.
For the lips of an immoral woman drip honey,
And her mouth is smoother than oil;
But in the end she is bitter as wormwood,
Sharp as a two-edged sword.
Her feet go down to death,
Her steps lay hold of hell.
Lest you ponder her path of life—
Her ways are unstable;
You do not know them.
Therefore hear me now, my children,
And do not depart from the words of my
  mouth.
Remove your way far from her,
And do not go near the door of her house,

Lest you give your honor to others,
And your years to the cruel one;
Lest aliens be filled with your wealth,
And your labors go to the house of a
    foreigner;
And you mourn at last,
When your flesh and your body are
    consumed,
And say:
"How I have hated instruction,
And my heart despised correction!
I have not obeyed the voice of my teachers,
Nor inclined my ear to those who instructed
    me!
I was on the verge of total ruin,
In the midst of the assembly and
    congregation."
Drink water from your own cistern,
And running water from your own well.
Should your fountains be dispersed abroad,
Streams of water in the streets?
Let them be only your own,
And not for strangers with you.
Let your fountain be blessed,
And rejoice with the wife of your youth.
As a loving deer and a graceful doe,
Let her breasts satisfy you at all times;
And always be enraptured with her love.
For why should you, my son, be enraptured
    by an immoral woman,
And be embraced in the arms of a seductress?

For the ways of man are before the eyes of the
    LORD,
And He ponders all his paths.

—PROVERBS 5:1–21

Can a man take fire to his bosom,
And his clothes not be burned?
Can one walk on hot coals,
And his feet not be seared?
So is he who goes in to his neighbor's wife;
Whoever touches her shall not be innocent.
People do not despise a thief
If he steals to satisfy himself when he is
    starving.
Yet when he is found, he must restore
    sevenfold;
He may have to give up all the substance of
    his house.
Whoever commits adultery with a woman
    lacks understanding;
He who does so destroys his own soul.
Wounds and dishonor he will get,
And his reproach will not be wiped away.

—PROVERBS 6:27–33

■ Approach Communion With Self-Examination

Therefore whoever eats this bread or drinks this
cup of the Lord in an unworthy manner will be
guilty of the body and blood of the Lord. But let a
man examine himself, and so let him eat of that

bread and drink of that cup. For he who eats and drinks in an unworthy manner eats and drinks judgment to himself, not discerning the Lord's body. For this reason many are weak and sick among you, and many sleep. For if we would judge ourselves, we would not be judged. But when we are judged, we are chastened by the Lord, that we may not be condemned with the world.

—1 CORINTHIANS 11:27-32

"And now, Lord, what do I wait for?
My hope is in You.
Deliver me from all my transgressions;
Do not make me the reproach of the foolish."

—PSALM 39:7-8

Have mercy upon me, O God,
According to Your lovingkindness;
According to the multitude of Your tender
    mercies,
Blot out my transgressions.
Wash me thoroughly from my iniquity,
And cleanse me from my sin.
Create in me a clean heart, O God,
And renew a steadfast spirit within me.

—PSALM 51:1-2, 10

God's Response

■ *God Rejoices in Repentance*

The Lord is not slack concerning His promise,
as some count slackness, but is longsuffering
toward us, not willing that any should perish but
that all should come to repentance.

—2 PETER 3:9

When I kept silent, my bones grew old
Through my groaning all the day long.
For day and night Your hand was heavy upon
   me;
My vitality was turned into the drought of
   summer.
I acknowledged my sin to You,
And my iniquity I have not hidden.
I said, "I will confess my transgressions to the
   LORD,"
And You forgave the iniquity of my sin.

—PSALM 32:3–5

"What man of you, having a hundred sheep, if
he loses one of them, does not leave the ninety-
nine in the wilderness, and go after the one which
is lost until he finds it? And when he has found it,
he lays it on his shoulders, rejoicing. And when he
comes home, he calls together his friends and
neighbors, saying to them, 'Rejoice with me, for I
have found my sheep which was lost!'

"I say to you that likewise there will be more joy in heaven over one sinner who repents than over ninety-nine just persons who need no repentance."

—LUKE 15:4–7

Then He said: "A certain man had two sons. And the younger of them said to his father, 'Father, give me the portion of goods that falls to me.' So he divided to them his livelihood.

"And not many days after, the younger son gathered all together, journeyed to a far country, and there wasted his possessions with prodigal living.

"But when he had spent all, there arose a severe famine in that land, and he began to be in want. Then he went and joined himself to a citizen of that country, and he sent him into his fields to feed swine. And he would gladly have filled his stomach with the pods that the swine ate, and no one gave him anything.

"But when he came to himself, he said, 'How many of my father's hired servants have bread enough and to spare, and I perish with hunger! I will arise and go to my father, and will say to him, "Father, I have sinned against heaven and before you, and I am no longer worthy to be called your son. Make me like one of your hired servants."'

"And he arose and came to his father. But when he was still a great way off, his father saw him and had compassion, and ran and fell on his neck and kissed him.

"And the son said to him, 'Father, I have sinned against heaven and in your sight, and am no longer worthy to be called your son.'

"But the father said to his servants, 'Bring out the best robe and put it on him, and put a ring on his hand and sandals on his feet. And bring the fatted calf here and kill it, and let us eat and be merry; for this my son was dead and is alive again; he was lost and is found.'"

—LUKE 15:11–24

■ God Lifts Me Up, Even After Failure

The steps of a good man are ordered by the
LORD,
And He delights in his way.
Though he fall, he shall not be utterly cast
down;
For the LORD upholds him with His hand.

—PSALM 37:23–24

"Because he has set his love upon Me,
therefore I will deliver him;
I will set him on high, because he has known
My name.
He shall call upon Me, and I will answer him;
I will be with him in trouble;
I will deliver him and honor him.
With long life I will satisfy him,
And show him My salvation."

—PSALM 91:14–16

Bless the LORD, O my soul,
And forget not all His benefits:
Who forgives all your iniquities,
Who heals all your diseases,
Who redeems your life from destruction,
Who crowns you with lovingkindness and
   tender mercies, Who satisfies your mouth
   with good things,
So that your youth is renewed like the eagle's.

—PSALM 103:2–5

THE
FUTURE

Higher Power: Will You Look to God for Strength?

A Russian cosmonaut once emerged from his spacecraft and stated that because he had not seen God in recent orbital travels, then surely God did not exist! Of course, we don't have to go into outer space if we want to deny the evidence for God. We can just as easily close our eyes to the miracle of creation, and of the existence of love itself, right where we are.

Yet people in recovery, who have at some point reached the "bottom" in one way or another, know that there is more to life than just what they can see and touch. There is, at the very least, an incredible, though perhaps not fully known, voice within them pointing out what they ought to do, asking them to turn and be accepted, seemingly wooing them into a relationship.

In the Bible, the apostle Paul spoke to a group of philosophers who had apparently heard that voice on occasion. He came across their "Unknown God" and told them this God is actually quite knowable!

Do you know this God? Would you like to know more? Read on . . .

The 'Unknown God': The One So Close to Us

■ *He Makes Himself Known to Us*

Then Paul stood in the midst of the Areopagus and said, "Men of Athens, I perceive that in all things you are very religious; for as I was passing through and considering the objects of your worship, I even found an altar with this inscription:

TO THE UNKNOWN GOD.

Therefore, the One whom you worship without knowing, Him I proclaim to you: God, who made the world and everything in it, since He is Lord of heaven and earth, does not dwell in temples made with hands. Nor is He worshiped with men's hands, as though He needed anything, since He gives to all life, breath, and all things. And He has made from one blood every nation of men to dwell on all the face of the earth, and has determined their preappointed times and the boundaries of their habitations, so that they should seek the Lord, in the hope that they might grope for Him and find Him, though He is not far from each one of us; for in Him we live and move and have our being, as also some of your own poets have said, 'For we are also His offspring.'

Therefore, since we are the offspring of God, we ought not to think that the Divine Nature is like gold or silver or stone, something shaped by art and man's devising. Truly, these times of ignorance God overlooked, but now commands all men everywhere to repent."

—ACTS 17:22–30

■ *He Knows Us Too*

O LORD, You have searched me and known
    me.
You know my sitting down and my rising up;
You understand my thought afar off.
You comprehend my path and my lying
    down,
And are acquainted with all my ways.
For there is not a word on my tongue,
But behold, O LORD, You know it altogether.
You have hedged me behind and before,
And laid Your hand upon me.
Such knowledge is too wonderful for me;
It is high, I cannot attain it.
Where can I go from Your Spirit?
Or where can I flee from Your presence?
If I ascend into heaven, You are there;
If I make my bed in hell, behold, You are
    there.
If I take the wings of the morning,

And dwell in the uttermost parts of the sea,
Even there Your hand shall lead me,
And Your right hand shall hold me.
If I say, "Surely the darkness shall fall on me,"
Even the night shall be light about me;
Indeed, the darkness shall not hide from You,
But the night shines as the day;
The darkness and the light are both alike to
    You.
For You have formed my inward parts;
You have covered me in my mother's womb.
I will praise You, for I am fearfully and
    wonderfully made;
Marvelous are Your works,
And that my soul knows very well.
My frame was not hidden from You,
When I was made in secret,
And skillfully wrought in the lowest parts of
    the earth.
Your eyes saw my substance, being yet
    unformed.
And in Your book they all were written,
The days fashioned for me,
When as yet there were none of them.

—PSALM 139:1–16

The Father: The One Who Made Us

I will praise You, for I am fearfully and
    wonderfully made;
Marvelous are Your works,

And that my soul knows very well.
My frame was not hidden from You,
When I was made in secret,
And skillfully wrought in the lowest parts of
    the earth.
Your eyes saw my substance, being yet
    unformed.
And in Your book they all were written,
The days fashioned for me,
When as yet there were none of them.

—PSALM 139:14–16

■ He Takes Care of All Who Trust Him

The LORD is my shepherd;
I shall not want.
He makes me to lie down in green pastures;
He leads me beside the still waters.
He restores my soul;
He leads me in the paths of righteousness
For His name's sake.
Yea, though I walk through the valley of the
    shadow of death,
I will fear no evil;
For You are with me;
Your rod and Your staff, they comfort me.
You prepare a table before me in the presence
    of my enemies;
You anoint my head with oil;
My cup runs over.
Surely goodness and mercy shall follow me
All the days of my life;

And I will dwell in the house of the LORD
Forever.

—PSALM 23:1–6

The LORD is my strength and my shield;
My heart trusted in Him, and I am helped;
Therefore my heart greatly rejoices,
And with my song I will praise Him.
The LORD is their strength,
And He is the saving refuge of His anointed.

—PSALM 28:7–8

He who dwells in the secret place of the Most
    High
Shall abide under the shadow of the Almighty.
I will say of the LORD, "He is my refuge and
    my fortress;
My God, in Him I will trust."
Surely He shall deliver you from the snare of
    the fowler
And from the perilous pestilence.
He shall cover you with His feathers,
And under His wings you shall take refuge;
His truth shall be your shield and buckler.

—PSALM 91:1–4

God is our refuge and strength,
A very present help in trouble.
Therefore we will not fear,
Though the earth be removed,
And though the mountains be carried into the
    midst of the sea;

Though its waters roar and be troubled,
Though the mountains shake with its
  swelling. Selah

—PSALM 46:1-3

In You, O LORD, I put my trust;
Let me never be put to shame.
Deliver me in Your righteousness, and cause
  me to escape;
Incline Your ear to me, and save me.
Be my strong habitation,
To which I may resort continually;
You have given the commandment to save me,
For You are my rock and my fortress.

—PSALM 71:1-3

■ *He Extends Goodness and Love*

Oh, how great is Your goodness,
Which You have laid up for those who fear
  You,
Which You have prepared for those who trust
  in You
In the presence of the sons of men!
You shall hide them in the secret place of Your
  presence
From the plots of man;
You shall keep them secretly in a pavilion
From the strife of tongues.

—PSALM 31:19-20

Oh, that men would give thanks to the LORD
 for His goodness,
And for His wonderful works to the children
 of men! . . .
Yet He sets the poor on high, far from
 affliction,
And makes their families like a flock.
The righteous see it and rejoice,
And all iniquity stops its mouth.
Whoever is wise will observe these things,
And they will understand the lovingkindness
 of the LORD.

—PSALM 107:31, 41–43

For I am persuaded that neither death nor life,
nor angels nor principalities nor powers, nor
things present nor things to come, nor height nor
depth, nor any other created thing, shall be able to
separate us from the love of God which is in Christ
Jesus our Lord.

—ROMANS 8:38–39

■ He Is Merciful

My merciful God shall come to meet me;
God shall let me see my desire on my
 enemies. . . .
But I will sing of Your power;
Yes, I will sing aloud of Your mercy in the
 morning; For You have been my defense
And refuge in the day of my trouble.

To You, O my Strength, I will sing praises;
For God is my defense, the God of my mercy.

—PSALM 59:10, 16–17

Also to You, O Lord, belongs mercy;
For You render to each one according to his work.

—PSALM 62:12

Has His mercy ceased forever?
Has His promise failed forevermore?
Has God forgotten to be gracious?
Has He in anger shut up His tender mercies? Selah

—PSALM 77:8–9

Oh, do not remember former iniquities against us!
Let Your tender mercies come speedily to meet us,
For we have been brought very low.

—PSALM 79:8

For You, Lord, are good, and ready to forgive,
And abundant in mercy to all those who call upon You.

—PSALM 86:5

For the LORD is good;
His mercy is everlasting,
And His truth endures to all generations.

—PSALM 100:5

The Son: The One Who Lived on Earth With Us

In the beginning was the Word, and the Word was with God, and the Word was God. He was in the beginning with God. All things were made through Him, and without Him nothing was made that was made. In Him was life, and the life was the light of men. . . .

He came to His own, and His own did not receive Him. But as many as received Him, to them He gave the right to become children of God, to those who believe in His name: who were born, not of blood, nor of the will of the flesh, nor of the will of man, but of God.

And the Word became flesh and dwelt among us, and we beheld His glory, the glory as of the only begotten of the Father, full of grace and truth.

—JOHN 1:1–4, 11–14

For in Him dwells all the fullness of the
   Godhead bodily.

—COLOSSIANS 2:9

■ He Is One with the Father

Then the Jews surrounded Him and said to Him, "How long do You keep us in doubt? If You are the Christ, tell us plainly."

Jesus answered them, "I told you, and you do not believe. The works that I do in My Father's name, they bear witness of Me. But you do not believe, because you are not of My sheep, as I said to you.

"My sheep hear My voice, and I know them, and they follow Me. And I give them eternal life, and they shall never perish; neither shall anyone snatch them out of My hand. My Father, who has given them to Me, is greater than all; and no one is able to snatch them out of My Father's hand.

"I and My Father are one."

Then the Jews took up stones again to stone Him.

Jesus answered them, "Many good works I have shown you from My Father. For which of those works do you stone Me?"

The Jews answered Him, saying, "For a good work we do not stone You, but for blasphemy, and because You, being a Man, make Yourself God."

Jesus answered them, "Is it not written in your law, 'I said, "You are gods"'? If He called them gods, to whom the word of God came (and the Scripture cannot be broken), do you say of Him whom the Father sanctified and sent into the world, 'You are blaspheming,' because I said, 'I am the Son of God'?

"If I do not do the works of My Father, do not believe Me; but if I do, though you do not believe Me, believe the works, that you may know and believe that the Father is in Me, and I in Him."

—JOHN 10:24–38

■ He Is the Way to the Father

Jesus said to him, "I am the way, the truth, and the life. No one comes to the Father except through Me."

—JOHN 14:6

"Nor is there salvation in any other, for there is no other name under heaven given among men by which we must be saved."

—ACTS 4:12

For He made Him who knew no sin to be sin for us, that we might become the righteousness of God in Him.

—2 CORINTHIANS 5:21

Who gave Himself for our sins, that He might deliver us from this present evil age, according to the will of our God and Father.

—GALATIANS 1:4

Inasmuch then as the children have partaken of flesh and blood, He Himself likewise shared in the same, that through death He might destroy him who had the power of death, that is, the devil, and release those who through fear of death were all their lifetime subject to bondage. For indeed He does not give aid to angels, but He does give aid to the seed of Abraham.

Therefore, in all things He had to be made like His brethren, that He might be a merciful and faithful High Priest in things pertaining to God, to make propitiation for the sins of the people. For in that He Himself has suffered, being tempted, He is able to aid those who are tempted.

—HEBREWS 2:14–18

■ He Is the Bread of Life

And Jesus said to them, "I am the bread of life. He who comes to Me shall never hunger, and he who believes in Me shall never thirst. But I said to you that you have seen Me and yet do not believe.

"All that the Father gives Me will come to Me, and the one who comes to Me I will by no means cast out. For I have come down from heaven, not to do My own will, but the will of Him who sent Me. This is the will of the Father who sent Me, that of all He has given Me I should lose nothing, but should raise it up at the last day. And this is the will of Him who sent Me, that everyone who sees the Son and believes in Him may have everlasting life; and I will raise him up at the last day."

—JOHN 6:35–40

■ He Is the Light of the World

Then Jesus spoke to them again, saying, "I am the light of the world. He who follows Me shall not walk in darkness, but have the light of life."

The Pharisees therefore said to Him, "You bear witness of Yourself; Your witness is not true."

Jesus answered and said to them, "Even if I bear

witness of Myself, My witness is true, for I know where I came from and where I am going; but you do not know where I come from and where I am going."

—JOHN 8:12-14

■ *He Is the Door, and the Good Shepherd*

Then Jesus said to them again, "Most assuredly, I say to you, I am the door of the sheep. All who ever came before Me are thieves and robbers, but the sheep did not hear them. I am the door. If anyone enters by Me, he will be saved, and will go in and out and find pasture.

"The thief does not come except to steal, and to kill, and to destroy. I have come that they may have life, and that they may have it more abundantly.

"I am the good shepherd. The good shepherd gives His life for the sheep. But he who is a hireling and not the shepherd, one who does not own the sheep, sees the wolf coming and leaves the sheep and flees; and the wolf catches the sheep and scatters them. The hireling flees because he is a hireling and does not care about the sheep.

"I am the good shepherd; and I know My sheep, and am known by My own. As the Father knows Me, even so I know the Father; and I lay down My life for the sheep. And other sheep I have which are not of this fold; them also I must bring, and they will hear My voice; and there will be one flock and one shepherd.

"Therefore My Father loves Me, because I lay down My life that I may take it again. No one takes it from Me, but I lay it down of Myself. I have power to lay it down, and I have power to take it again. This command I have received from My Father."

—JOHN 10:7–18

■ He Is the Resurrection and the Life

Then Martha said to Jesus, "Lord, if You had been here, my brother would not have died. But even now I know that whatever You ask of God, God will give You."

Jesus said to her, "Your brother will rise again."

Martha said to Him, "I know that he will rise again in the resurrection at the last day."

Jesus said to her, "I am the resurrection and the life. He who believes in Me, though he may die, he shall live. And whoever lives and believes in Me shall never die. Do you believe this?"

—JOHN 11:21–26

■ He Is the Vine

"I am the true vine, and My Father is the vinedresser. Every branch in Me that does not bear fruit He takes away; and every branch that bears fruit He prunes, that it may bear more fruit.

"You are already clean because of the word which I have spoken to you. Abide in Me, and I in you. As the branch cannot bear fruit of itself, unless it abides in the vine, neither can you, unless you abide in Me.

"I am the vine, you are the branches. He who abides in Me, and I in him, bears much fruit; for without Me you can do nothing. If anyone does not abide in Me, he is cast out as a branch and is withered; and they gather them and throw them into the fire, and they are burned. If you abide in Me, and My words abide in you, you will ask what you desire, and it shall be done for you."

—JOHN 15:1–7

The Holy Spirit: The One Who Dwells Inside Us

For there are three that bear witness in heaven: the Father, the Word, and the Holy Spirit; and these three are one.

—1 JOHN 5:7

■ He Helps and Teaches Us

Jesus answered and said to him, "If anyone loves Me, he will keep My word; and My Father will love him, and We will come to him and make Our home with him. He who does not love Me does not keep My words; and the word which you hear is not Mine but the Father's who sent Me. These things I have spoken to you while being present with you. But the Helper, the Holy Spirit, whom the Father will send in My name, He will teach you all things, and bring to your remembrance all things that I said to you."

—JOHN 14:23–26

■ *He Convicts Us of Sin*

"But now I go away to Him who sent Me, and none of you asks Me, 'Where are You going?' But because I have said these things to you, sorrow has filled your heart. Nevertheless I tell you the truth. It is to your advantage that I go away; for if I do not go away, the Helper will not come to you; but if I depart, I will send Him to you.

"And when He has come, He will convict the world of sin, and of righteousness, and of judgment: of sin, because they do not believe in Me; of righteousness, because I go to My Father and you see Me no more; of judgment, because the ruler of this world is judged.

"I still have many things to say to you, but you cannot bear them now. However, when He, the Spirit of truth, has come, He will guide you into all truth; for He will not speak on His own authority, but whatever He hears He will speak; and He will tell you things to come. He will glorify Me, for He will take of what is Mine and declare it to you.

"All things that the Father has are Mine. Therefore I said that He will take of Mine and declare it to you."

—JOHN 16:5–15

■ *He Leads Us into Holy Living*

There is therefore now no condemnation to those who are in Christ Jesus, who do not walk according to the flesh, but according to the Spirit. For the law of the Spirit of life in Christ Jesus has made me free from the law of sin and death. For what the law could not do in that it was weak through the flesh, God did by sending His own Son in the likeness of sinful flesh, on account of sin: He condemned sin in the flesh, that the righteous requirement of the law might be fulfilled in us who do not walk according to the flesh but according to the Spirit.

For those who live according to the flesh set their minds on the things of the flesh, but those who live according to the Spirit, the things of the Spirit. For to be carnally minded is death, but to be spiritually minded is life and peace. Because the carnal mind is enmity against God; for it is not subject to the law of God, nor indeed can be.

So then, those who are in the flesh cannot please God. But you are not in the flesh but in the Spirit, if indeed the Spirit of God dwells in you. Now if anyone does not have the Spirit of Christ, he is not His. And if Christ is in you, the body is dead because of sin, but the Spirit is life because of righteousness. But if the Spirit of Him who raised Jesus from the dead dwells in you, He who raised Christ from the dead will also give life to your mortal bodies through His Spirit who dwells in you.

Therefore, brethren, we are debtors—not to the flesh, to live according to the flesh. For if you live according to the flesh you will die; but if by the Spirit you put to death the deeds of the body, you will live. For as many as are led by the Spirit of God, these are sons of God.

—ROMANS 8:1–14

■ He Helps Us Pray

Likewise the Spirit also helps in our weaknesses. For we do not know what we should pray for as we ought, but the Spirit Himself makes intercession for us with groanings which cannot be uttered. Now He who searches the hearts knows what the mind of the Spirit is, because He makes intercession for the saints according to the will of God.

—ROMANS 8:26–27

CHAPTER 8

Spiritual Life: Will You Seek New Avenues of Nurture?

The life of the spirit is hard to nail down. But we know when we are encouraging it, and we know when we are letting it get away from us. For instance, after hectic weeks of involvement with purely practical concerns—daily work routines, family responsibilities, community events—we may come to a moment of solitude and realize: I have not been with myself, not really. I have not had a chance to know my thoughts; nor have I been with my God, or considered His thoughts. My spirit has shriveled a bit! I need to let it blossom again.

What better way to move into the future than with a vibrant spiritual life? The Scriptures suggest that this is not a way of building a new discipline into our lives (with all the potential for failure that can bring). Rather, it is a call to find new ways to fill up our love-hunger tanks through prayer, worship, and doing good toward others. The great promise is that all these things move us into a more peaceful way of living.

Ask God for Vibrant Spiritual Life

And He said to them, "Which of you shall have a friend, and go to him at midnight and say to him, 'Friend, lend me three loaves; for a friend of mine has come to me on his journey, and I have nothing to set before him'; and he will answer from within and say, 'Do not trouble me; the door is now shut, and my children are with me in bed; I cannot rise and give to you'?

"I say to you, though he will not rise and give to him because he is his friend, yet because of his persistence he will rise and give him as many as he needs. So I say to you, ask, and it will be given to you; seek, and you will find; knock, and it will be opened to you. For everyone who asks receives, and he who seeks finds, and to him who knocks it will be opened."

—LUKE 11:5–10

Out of the depths I have cried to You, O
    LORD; Lord, hear my voice!
Let Your ears be attentive
To the voice of my supplications.
If You, LORD, should mark iniquities,
O Lord, who could stand?
But there is forgiveness with You,

That You may be feared.
I wait for the LORD, my soul waits,
And in His word I do hope.
My soul waits for the Lord
More than those who watch for the morning—
I say more than those who watch for the
morning.

—PSALM 130:1–6

"Come to Me, all you who labor and are heavy laden, and I will give you rest. Take My yoke upon you and learn from Me, for I am gentle and lowly in heart, and you will find rest for your souls. For My yoke is easy and My burden is light."

—MATTHEW 11:28–30

For by grace you have been saved through faith, and that not of yourselves; it is the gift of God, not of works, lest anyone should boast.

—EPHESIANS 2:8–9

Take Up the Challenge of the Spiritual Life

"He who loves father or mother more than Me is not worthy of Me. And he who loves son or daughter more than Me is not worthy of Me. And he who does not take his cross and follow after Me is not worthy of Me. He who finds his life will lose it, and he who loses his life for My sake will find it."

—MATTHEW 10:37–39

Now it happened as they journeyed on the road, that someone said to Him, "Lord, I will follow You wherever You go." And Jesus said to him, "Foxes have holes and birds of the air have nests, but the Son of Man has nowhere to lay His head."

Then He said to another, "Follow Me." But he said, "Lord, let me first go and bury my father." Jesus said to him, "Let the dead bury their own dead, but you go and preach the kingdom of God."

And another also said, "Lord, I will follow You, but let me first go and bid them farewell who are at my house." But Jesus said to him, "No one, having put his hand to the plow, and looking back, is fit for the kingdom of God."

—LUKE 9:57-62

■ *Find Delight in the Scriptures*

All Scripture is given by inspiration of God, and is profitable for doctrine, for reproof, for correction, for instruction in righteousness, that the man of God may be complete, thoroughly equipped for every good work.

—2 TIMOTHY 3:16-17

Blessed is the man
Who walks not in the counsel of the ungodly,
Nor stands in the path of sinners,
Nor sits in the seat of the scornful;
But his delight is in the law of the LORD,
And in His law he meditates day and night.

He shall be like a tree
Planted by the rivers of water,
That brings forth its fruit in its season,
Whose leaf also shall not wither;
And whatever he does shall prosper.

—PSALM 1:1–3

Your word I have hidden in my heart,
That I might not sin against You! . . .
I will delight myself in Your statutes;
I will not forget Your word. . . .
So shall I have an answer for him who
    reproaches me, For I trust in Your word. . . .
This is my comfort in my affliction,
For Your word has given me life. . . .
Your word is a lamp to my feet
And a light to my path.

—PSALM 119: 11, 16, 42, 50, 105

■ Find Comfort in Prayer

Is anyone among you suffering? Let him pray. Is anyone cheerful? Let him sing psalms. Is anyone among you sick? Let him call for the elders of the church, and let them pray over him, anointing him with oil in the name of the Lord. And the prayer of faith will save the sick, and the Lord will raise him up. And if he has committed sins, he will be forgiven.

Confess your trespasses to one another, and pray for one another, that you may be healed. The effective, fervent prayer of a righteous man avails much. Elijah was a man with a nature like ours, and he prayed earnestly that it would not rain; and it did not rain on the land for three years and six months. And he prayed again, and the heaven gave rain, and the earth produced its fruit.

—JAMES 5:13–18

"For the eyes of the LORD are on the
   righteous,
And his ears are open to their prayers;
But the face of the LORD is against those who
   do evil."

—1 PETER 3:12

Therefore by Him let us continually offer the sacrifice of praise to God, that is, the fruit of our lips, giving thanks to His name.

—HEBREWS 13:15

Then He said to them, "Why do you sleep? Rise and pray, lest you enter into temptation."

—LUKE 22:46

But the end of all things is at hand; therefore be serious and watchful in your prayers.

—1 PETER 4:7

Pray without ceasing.

—1 THESSALONIANS 5:17

Therefore I exhort first of all that supplications, prayers, intercessions, and giving of thanks be made for all men. . . . Therefore I desire that the men pray everywhere, lifting up holy hands, without wrath and doubting.

—1 TIMOTHY 2:1, 8

Be anxious for nothing, but in everything by prayer and supplication, with thanksgiving, let your requests be made known to God.

—PHILIPPIANS 4:6

Likewise the Spirit also helps in our weaknesses. For we do not know what we should pray for as we ought, but the Spirit Himself makes intercession for us with groanings which cannot be uttered. Now He who searches the hearts knows what the mind of the Spirit is, because He makes intercession for the saints according to the will of God. And we know that all things work together for good to those who love God, to those who are the called according to His purpose.

—ROMANS 8:26–28

■ *Find Meaning in Worship*

Oh, give thanks to the LORD!
Call upon His name;
Make known His deeds among the peoples!
Sing to Him, sing psalms to Him;
Talk of all His wondrous works.
Glory in His holy name;

Let the hearts of those rejoice who seek the
  LORD!
Seek the LORD and His strength;
Seek His face evermore.

—PSALM 105:1–4

Jesus said to her, "Woman, believe Me, the hour
is coming when you will neither on this mountain,
nor in Jerusalem, worship the Father. You worship
what you do not know; we know what we worship, for salvation is of the Jews. But the hour is
coming, and now is, when the true worshipers
will worship the Father in spirit and truth; for the
Father is seeking such to worship Him. God is
Spirit, and those who worship Him must worship
in spirit and truth."

—JOHN 4:21–24

"Fear God and give glory to Him, for the hour of
His judgment has come; and worship Him who
made heaven and earth, the sea and springs of water."

—REVELATION 14:7

"Who shall not fear You, O Lord, and glorify
  Your name?
For You alone are holy.
For all nations shall come and worship before
  You,
For Your judgments have been manifested."

—REVELATION 15:4

■ Find Fulfillment in Doing Good

But be doers of the word, and not hearers only, deceiving yourselves. For if anyone is a hearer of the word and not a doer, he is like a man observing his natural face in a mirror; for he observes himself, goes away, and immediately forgets what kind of man he was. But he who looks into the perfect law of liberty and continues in it, and is not a forgetful hearer but a doer of the work, this one will be blessed in what he does. . . .

Pure and undefiled religion before God and the Father is this: to visit orphans and widows in their trouble, and to keep oneself unspotted from the world.

—JAMES 1:22–25, 27

■ Find Purpose in Complete Dedication

For to me, to live is Christ, and to die is gain.
—PHILIPPIANS 1:21

But what things were gain to me, these I have counted loss for Christ. But indeed I also count all things loss for the excellence of the knowledge of Christ Jesus my Lord, for whom I have suffered the loss of all things, and count them as rubbish, that I may gain Christ and be found in Him, not having my own righteousness, which is from the law, but that which is through faith in Christ, the righteousness which is from God by faith; that I may know Him and the power of His resurrection,

and the fellowship of His sufferings, being conformed to His death, if, by any means, I may attain
to the resurrection from the dead. Not that I have
already attained, or am already perfected; but I
press on, that I may lay hold of that for which
Christ Jesus has also laid hold of me.

Brethren, I do not count myself to have appre-
hended; but one thing I do, forgetting those
things which are behind and reaching forward to
those things which are ahead, I press toward the
goal for the prize of the upward call of God in
Christ Jesus.

—PHILIPPIANS 3:7–14

As you have therefore received Christ Jesus the
Lord, so walk in Him, rooted and built up in Him
and established in the faith, as you have been
taught, abounding in it with thanksgiving. Beware
lest anyone cheat you through philosophy and
empty deceit, according to the tradition of men,
according to the basic principles of the world, and
not according to Christ. For in Him dwells all the
fullness of the Godhead bodily; and you are complete in Him, who is the head of all principality
and power.

—COLOSSIANS 2:6–10

■ Find Soul-Nourishment in the Lord's Supper

And as they were eating, Jesus took bread,
blessed it and broke it, and gave it to the disciples
and said, "Take, eat; this is My body." Then He

took the cup, and gave thanks, and gave it to them, saying, "Drink from it, all of you. For this is My blood of the new covenant, which is shed for many for the remission of sins."

—MATTHEW 26:26–28

"Do not labor for the food which perishes, but for the food which endures to everlasting life, which the Son of Man will give you, because God the Father has set His seal on Him." . . .

Then Jesus said to them, "Most assuredly, I say to you, Moses did not give you the bread from heaven, but My Father gives you the true bread from heaven. For the bread of God is He who comes down from heaven and gives life to the world."

Then they said to Him, "Lord, give us this bread always."

And Jesus said to them, "I am the bread of life. He who comes to Me shall never hunger, and he who believes in Me shall never thirst. . . .

"I am the living bread which came down from heaven. If anyone eats of this bread, he will live forever; and the bread that I shall give is My flesh, which I shall give for the life of the world."

The Jews therefore quarreled among themselves, saying, "How can this Man give us His flesh to eat?"

Then Jesus said to them, "Most assuredly, I say to you, unless you eat the flesh of the Son of Man and drink His blood, you have no life in you. Whoever eats My flesh and drinks My blood has eternal life, and I will raise him up at the last day. For My flesh is food indeed, and My blood is drink indeed.

"He who eats My flesh and drinks My blood abides in Me, and I in him. As the living Father sent Me, and I live because of the Father, so he who feeds on Me will live because of Me.

"This is the bread which came down from heaven—not as your fathers ate the manna, and are dead. He who eats this bread will live forever."

—JOHN 6:27, 32–35, 51–58

For as often as you eat this bread and drink this cup, you proclaim the Lord's death till He comes.

—1 CORINTHIANS 11:26

Rest in God's Inner Peace

You will keep him in perfect peace,
Whose mind is stayed on You,
Because he trusts in You.

—ISAIAH 26:3

For he shall be like a tree planted by the
    waters,
Which spreads out its roots by the river,
And will not fear when heat comes;
But her leaf will be green,
And will not be anxious in the year of
    drought,
Nor will cease from yielding fruit.

—JEREMIAH 17:8

"Peace I leave with you, My peace I give to you; not as the world gives do I give to you. Let not your heart be troubled, neither let it be afraid."

—JOHN 14:27

"These things I have spoken to you, that in Me you may have peace. In the world you will have tribulation; but be of good cheer, I have overcome the world."

—JOHN 16:33

For God is not the author of confusion but of peace, as in all the churches of the saints.

—1 CORINTHIANS 14:33

For He Himself is our peace, who has made both one, and has broken down the middle wall of division between us, having abolished in His flesh the enmity, that is, the law of commandments contained in ordinances, so as to create in Himself one new man from the two, thus making peace. . . .

And He came and preached peace to you who were afar off and to those who were near.

—EPHESIANS 2:14–15, 17

The peace of God, which surpasses all understanding, will guard your hearts and minds through Christ Jesus.

—PHILIPPIANS 4:7

Now may the Lord of peace Himself give you peace always in every way. The Lord be with you all.

—2 THESSALONIANS 3:16

Resist the Power of the Enemy

Be sober, be vigilant; because your adversary the devil walks about like a roaring lion, seeking whom he may devour.

—1 PETER 5:8

For though we walk in the flesh, we do not war according to the flesh. For the weapons of our warfare are not carnal but mighty in God for pulling down strongholds, casting down arguments and every high thing that exalts itself against the knowledge of God, bringing every thought into captivity to the obedience of Christ.

—2 CORINTHIANS 10:3–5

Put on the whole armor of God, that you may be able to stand against the wiles of the devil. For we do not wrestle against flesh and blood, but against principalities, against powers, against the rulers of the darkness of this age, against spiritual hosts of wickedness in the heavenly places. Therefore take up the whole armor of God, that you may be able to withstand in the evil day, and having done all, to stand.

Stand therefore, having girded your waist with truth, having put on the breastplate of righteousness, and having shod your feet with the preparation of the gospel of peace; above all, taking the shield of faith with which you will be able to quench all the fiery darts of the wicked one. And take the helmet of salvation, and the sword of the Spirit, which is the word of God; praying always with all prayer and supplication in the Spirit, being watchful to this end with all perseverance and supplication for all the saints.

—EPHESIANS 6:11–18

Freedom: Will You Continue to Take Care of Yourself?

What will it really mean for us to be free from the past? It certainly does not mean denying all that has occurred in our personal histories. That follows us to the end. And it certainly cannot mean that we let go of all past relationships that still have rightful claim on us even today. We can't just walk away from the past.

But perhaps we can walk away from old habits. This is recovery in a nutshell: Not changing the past's performance, but changing the future person. The key is to be very intentional about it, to recognize that if we don't take care of ourselves, then no one will. Without adequate self-care, we are vulnerable to old habits.

Therefore, it is my solemn responsibility to take care of me. To set reasonable limits on my commitments. To rely on God to see me through.

Taking Care of Myself

■ *Rest*

Then the apostles gathered to Jesus and told Him all things, both what they had done and what they had taught. And He said to them, "Come aside by yourselves to a deserted place and rest a while." For there were many coming and going, and they did not even have time to eat. So they departed to a deserted place in the boat by themselves.

—MARK 6:30–32

Six days you shall do your work, and on the seventh day you shall rest.

—EXODUS 23:12a

■ *Exercise*

When you walk, your steps will not be
    hindered,
And when you run, you will not stumble.

—PROVERBS 4:12

For by You I can run against a troop;
By my God I can leap over a wall.

—2 SAMUEL 22:30

He gives power to the weak,
And to those who have no might He increases
    strength.

Even the youths shall faint and be weary,
And the young men shall utterly fall,
But those who wait on the LORD
Shall renew their strength;
They shall mount up with wings like eagles,
They shall run and not be weary,
They shall walk and not faint.

—ISAIAH 40:29–31

I beseech you therefore, brethren, by the mercies of God, that you present your bodies a living sacrifice, holy, acceptable to God, which is your reasonable service.

—ROMANS 12:1

Or do you not know that your body is the temple of the Holy Spirit who is in you, whom you have from God, and you are not your own? For you were bought at a price; therefore glorify God in your body and in your spirit, which are God's.

—1 CORINTHIANS 6:19–20

For our citizenship is in heaven, from which we also eagerly wait for the Savior, the Lord Jesus Christ, who will transform our lowly body that it may be conformed to His glorious body, according to the working by which He is able even to subdue all things to Himself.

—PHILIPPIANS 3:20–21

■ Nutrition

In the multitude of my anxieties within me,
Your comforts delight my soul.

—PSALM 94:19

There is nothing is better for a man than that he
should eat and drink, and that his soul should enjoy good in his labor. This also, I saw, was from
the hand of God.

—ECCLESIASTES 2:24

Here is what I have seen: It is good and fitting
for one to eat and drink, and to enjoy the good of
all his labor in which he toils under the sun all the
days of his life which God gives him; for it is his
heritage. As for every man to whom God has
given riches and wealth, and given him power to
eat of it, to receive his heritage and rejoice in his
labor—this is the gift of God.

—ECCLESIASTES 5:18–19

■ Sleep

I lay down and slept;
I awoke, for the LORD sustained me.

—PSALM 3:5

Meditate within your heart on your bed, and
    be still.
Offer the sacrifices of righteousness,
And put your trust in the LORD.

There are many who say,
"Who will show us any good?"
LORD, lift up the light of Your countenance
  upon us.
You have put gladness in my heart,
More than in the season that their grain and
  wine increased.
I will both lie down in peace, and sleep;
For You alone, O LORD, make me dwell in
  safety.

—PSALM 4:4–8

Now when [Jesus] got into a boat, His disciples
followed Him. And suddenly a great tempest
arose on the sea, so that the boat was covered with
the waves. But He was asleep.

—MATTHEW 8:23–24

■ *Friends*

Faithful are the wounds of a friend,
But the kisses of an enemy are deceitful.

—PROVERBS 27:6

Ointment and perfume delight the heart,
And the sweetness of a man's friend does so
  by hearty counsel.
Do not forsake your own friend or your
  father's friend,
Nor go to your brother's house in the day of
  your calamity;

For better is a neighbor nearby than a brother
   far away.

—PROVERBS 27:9-10

Therefore comfort each other and edify one another, just as you also are doing.

—1 THESSALONIANS 5:11

Now we exhort you, brethren, warn those who
are unruly, comfort the fainthearted, uphold the
weak, be patient with all.

—1 THESSALONIANS 5:14

Not forsaking the assembling of ourselves together, as is the manner of some, but exhorting
one another, and so much the more as you see the
Day approaching.

—HEBREWS 10:25

Setting New Personal Boundaries

■ Relationships

"Moreover if your brother sins against you, go
and tell him his fault between you and him alone.
If he hears you, you have gained your brother. But
if he will not hear you, take with you one or two
more, that 'by the mouth of two or three witnesses
every word may be established.'

"And if he refuses to hear them, tell it to the
church. But if he refuses even to hear the church,

let him be to you like a heathen and a tax collector."

—MATTHEW 18:15–17

Therefore, putting away lying, each one speak truth with his neighbor, for we are members of one another.

—EPHESIANS 4:25

■ Sex

For at the window of my house
I looked through my lattice,
And saw among the simple,
I perceived among the youths,
A young man devoid of understanding,
Passing along the street near her corner;
And he took the path to her house
In the twilight, in the evening,
In the black and dark night.
And there a woman met him,
With the attire of a harlot, and a crafty heart.
She was loud and rebellious,
Her feet would not stay at home.
At times she was outside, at times in the open
    square,
Lurking at every corner.
So she caught him and kissed him;
With an impudent face she said to him:
"I have peace offerings with me;
Today I have paid my vows.
So I came out to meet you,

Diligently to seek your face,
And I have found you.
I have spread my bed with tapestry,
Colored coverings of Egyptian linen.
I have perfumed my bed
With myrrh, aloes, and cinnamon.
Come, let us take our fill of love until
    morning;
Let us delight ourselves with love.
For my husband is not at home;
He has gone on a long journey;
He has taken a bag of money with him,
And will come home on the appointed day."
With her enticing speech she caused him to
    yield,
With her flattering lips she seduced him.
Immediately he went after her, as an ox goes
    to the slaughter,
Or as a fool to the correction of the stocks.

—PROVERBS 7:6–22

■ Money

Now Jesus sat opposite the treasury and saw
how the people put money into the treasury. And
many who were rich put in much. Then one poor
widow came and threw in two mites, which make
a quadrans. So He called His disciples to Him and
said to them, "Assuredly, I say to you that this
poor widow has put in more than all those who
have given to the treasury; for they all put in out of

their abundance, but she out of her poverty put in all that she had, her whole livelihood."

—MARK 12:41–44

"Do not fear, little flock, for it is your Father's good pleasure to give you the kingdom. Sell what you have and give alms; provide yourselves money bags which do not grow old, a treasure in the heavens that does not fail, where no thief approaches nor moth destroys. For where your treasure is, there your heart will be also."

—LUKE 12:32–34

But godliness with contentment is great gain. For we brought nothing into this world, and it is certain we can carry nothing out. And having food and clothing, with these we shall be content. But those who desire to be rich fall into temptation and a snare, and into many foolish and harmful lusts which drown men in destruction and perdition. For the love of money is a root of all kinds of evil, for which some have strayed from the faith in their greediness, and pierced themselves through with many sorrows. But you, O man of God, flee these things and pursue righteousness, godliness, faith, love, patience, gentleness.

—1 TIMOTHY 6:6–11

■ Food and Drink

For none of us lives to himself, and no one dies to himself. For if we live, we live to the Lord; and if we die, we die to the Lord. Therefore, whether we live or die, we are the Lord's. For to this end Christ died and rose and lived again, that He might be Lord of both the dead and the living. . . .

So then each of us shall give account of himself to God. Therefore let us not judge one another anymore, but rather resolve this, not to put a stumbling block or a cause to fall in our brother's way. I know and am convinced by the Lord Jesus that there is nothing unclean of itself; but to him who considers anything to be unclean, to him it is unclean. . . . for the kingdom of God is not food and drink, but righteousness and peace and joy in the Holy Spirit. . . .

It is good neither to eat meat nor drink wine nor do anything by which your brother stumbles or is offended or is made weak.

—ROMANS 14:7–9, 12–14, 17, 21

Looking to the Future

■ *Walking In a New Way*

Walk in the Spirit, and you shall not fulfill the lust of the flesh. For the flesh lusts against the Spirit, and the Spirit against the flesh; and these are contrary to one another, so that you do not do the things that you wish.

—GALATIANS 5:16–17

This I say, therefore, and testify in the Lord, that you should no longer walk as the rest of the Gentiles walk, in the futility of their mind, having their understanding darkened, being alienated from the life of God, because of the ignorance that is in them, because of the hardening of their heart; who, being past feeling, have given themselves over to licentiousness, to work all uncleanness with greediness. But you have not so learned Christ, if indeed you have heard Him and have been taught by Him, as the truth is in Jesus: that you put off, concerning your former conduct, the old man which grows corrupt according to the deceitful lusts, and be renewed in the spirit of your mind. . . . For you were once darkness, but now you are light in the Lord. Walk as children of light (for the fruit of the Spirit is in all goodness, righteousness, and truth), proving what is acceptable to the Lord.

—EPHESIANS 4:17–23; 5:9–10

And do this, knowing the time, that now it is high time to awake out of sleep; for now our salvation is nearer than when we first believed. The night is far spent, the day is at hand. Therefore let us cast off the works of darkness, and let us put on the armor of light. Let us walk properly, as in the day, not in revelry and drunkenness, not in licentiousness and lewdness, not in strife and envy. But put on the Lord Jesus Christ, and make no provision for the flesh, to fulfill its lusts.

—ROMANS 13:11–14

For we have spent enough of our past lifetime in doing the will of the Gentiles—when we walked in licentiousness, lusts, drunkenness, revelries, drinking parties, and abominable idolatries.

—1 PETER 4:3

■ *Seeking Daily Help from God*

I will lift up my eyes to the hills—
From whence comes my help?
My help comes from the LORD,
Who made heaven and earth.
He will not allow your foot to be moved;
He who keeps you will not slumber.
Behold, He who keeps Israel
Shall neither slumber nor sleep.
The LORD is your keeper;
The LORD is your shade at your right hand.
The sun shall not strike you by day,
Nor the moon by night.
The LORD shall preserve you from all evil;
He shall preserve your soul.
The LORD shall preserve your going out and
   your coming in
From this time forth, and even forevermore.

—PSALM 121

O God, do not be far from me;
O my God, make haste to help me!
Let them be confounded and consumed
Who are adversaries of my life;

Let them be covered with reproach and
     dishonor
Who seek my hurt.
But I will hope continually,
And will praise You yet more and more.
My mouth shall tell of Your righteousness
And Your salvation all the day,
For I do not know their limits.
I will go in the strength of the Lord GOD;
I will make mention of Your righteousness, of
     Yours only.
O God, You have taught me from my youth;
And to this day I declare Your wondrous
     works.
Now also when I am old and grayheaded,
O God, do not forsake me,
Until I declare Your strength to this
     generation,
Your power to everyone who is to come.
Also Your righteousness, O God, is very high,
You who have done great things;
O God, who is like You?

—PSALM 71:12–19

Seeing then that we have a great High Priest
who has passed through the heavens, Jesus the
Son of God, let us hold fast our confession. For we
do not have a High Priest who cannot sympathize
with our weaknesses, but was in all points
tempted as we are, yet without sin. Let us therefore come boldly to the throne of grace, that we

may obtain mercy and find grace to help in time of need.

—HEBREWS 4:14–16

■ *Walking in the Shadow of God's Care*

The LORD is your keeper;
The LORD is your shade at your right hand.
The sun shall not strike you by day,
Nor the moon by night.
The LORD shall preserve you from all evil;
He shall preserve your soul.
The LORD shall preserve your going out and
    your coming in
From this time forth, and even forevermore.

—PSALM 121:5–8

CHAPTER 10

Carrying the Recovery Message to Others

Jesus said it to a man He had just healed:
Go home and tell about God's goodness to
you.

What about you? Have you experienced
some healing? How did it happen? Was it all
your doing? Or can you give a word of recom-
mendation to your Higher Power?

"You can't keep it unless you give it away."
The ultimate paradox! Yet we know it's true.
Ultimately, we want happiness. But we know
it will only come when we release our white-
knuckled grasp on what we think will get it for
us (name your addiction here: _____)
and turn our attention to making the lives of
others a little more happy.

Thanking God for My Own 'Spiritual Awakening'

It is good to give thanks to the LORD,
And to sing praises to Your name, O Most
   High;
To declare Your lovingkindness in the
   morning,
And Your faithfulness every night,
On an instrument of ten strings,
On the lute,
And on the harp,
With harmonious sound.
For You, LORD, have made me glad through
   Your work;
I will triumph in the works of Your hands.

                —PSALM 92:1–4

Oh, sing to the LORD a new song!
Sing to the LORD, all the earth.
Sing to the LORD, bless His name;
Proclaim the good news of His salvation from
   day to day.

                —PSALM 96:1–2

Praise the LORD!
Oh, give thanks to the LORD, for He is good!
For His mercy endures forever.
Who can utter the mighty acts of the LORD?
Or can declare all His praise?

Blessed are those who keep justice,
And he who does righteousness at all times!
—PSALM 106:1–3

Oh, give thanks to the LORD, for He is good!
For His mercy endures forever.
Let the redeemed of the LORD say so,
Whom He has redeemed from the hand of the
   enemy.
—PSALM 107:1–2

Oh, that men would give thanks to the LORD
   for His goodness,
And for His wonderful works to the children
   of men!
Let them sacrifice the sacrifices of
   thanksgiving,
And declare His works with rejoicing.
—PSALM 107:21–22

Praise the LORD!
I will praise the LORD with my whole heart,
In the assembly of the upright and in the
   congregation.
The works of the LORD are great,
Studied by all who have pleasure in them.
His work is honorable and glorious,
And His righteousness endures forever.
He has made His wonderful works to be
   remembered;
The LORD is gracious and full of compassion.

He has given food to those who fear Him;
He will ever be mindful of His covenant.
He has declared to His people the power of
    His works,
In giving them the heritage of the nations.
The works of His hands are verity and justice;
All His precepts are sure.
They stand fast forever and ever,
And are done in truth and uprightness.
He has sent redemption to His people;
He has commanded His covenant forever:
Holy and awesome is His name.
The fear of the LORD is the beginning of
    wisdom;
A good understanding have all those who do
    His commandments.
His praise endures forever.

—PSALM 111:1–10

I will extol You, my God, O King;
And I will bless Your name forever and ever.
Every day I will bless You,
And I will praise Your name forever and ever.
Great is the LORD, and greatly to be praised;
And His greatness is unsearchable.
One generation shall praise Your works to
    another,
And shall declare Your mighty acts.
I will meditate on the glorious splendor of
    Your majesty,
And on Your wondrous works.

Men shall speak of the might of Your awesome
   acts,
And I will declare Your greatness.
They shall utter the memory of Your great
   goodness,
And shall sing of Your righteousness.
The LORD is gracious and full of compassion,
Slow to anger and great in mercy.
The LORD is good to all,
And His tender mercies are over all His
   works.
All Your works shall praise You, O LORD,
And Your saints shall bless You.
They shall speak of the glory of Your
   kingdom,
And talk of Your power,
To make known to the sons of men His
   mighty acts, And the glorious majesty of
   His kingdom. . . .
My mouth shall speak the praise of the LORD,
And all flesh shall bless His holy name
Forever and ever.

—PSALM 145:1–12, 21

And I thank Christ Jesus our Lord who has en-
abled me, because He counted me faithful, putting me into the ministry, although I was formerly
a blasphemer, a persecutor, and an insolent man;
but I obtained mercy because I did it ignorantly in
unbelief. And the grace of our Lord was exceedingly abundant, with faith and love which are in

Christ Jesus. This is a faithful saying and worthy of all acceptance, that Christ Jesus came into the world to save sinners, of whom I am chief. However, for this reason I obtained mercy, that in me first Jesus Christ might show all longsuffering, as a pattern to those who are going to believe on Him for everlasting life.

—1 TIMOTHY 1:12–16

Befriending Those Looking for What's Missing

Out of the depths I have cried to You, O
    LORD;
Lord, hear my voice!
Let Your ears be attentive
To the voice of my supplications.
If You, LORD, should mark iniquities,
O Lord, who could stand?
But there is forgiveness with You,
That You may be feared.
I wait for the LORD, my soul waits,
And in His word I do hope.
My soul waits for the Lord
More than those who watch for the morning—
I say, more than those who watch for the
    morning.

—PSALM 130:1–6

I cry out to the LORD with my voice;
With my voice to the LORD I make my
    supplication.

I pour out my complaint before Him;
I declare before Him my trouble.
When my spirit was overwhelmed within me,
Then You knew my path.
In the way in which I walk
They have secretly set a snare for me.
Look on my right hand and see,
For there is no one who acknowledges me;
Refuge has failed me;
No one cares for my soul.

—PSALM 142:1–4

■ *God Can Fill Their Emptiness*

Come to Me, all you who labor and are heavy
laden, and I will give you rest. Take My yoke upon
you and learn from Me, for I am gentle and lowly
in heart, and you will find rest for your souls. For
My yoke is easy and My burden is light.

—MATTHEW 11:28–30

On the last day, that great day of the feast, Jesus
stood and cried out, saying, "If anyone thirsts, let
him come to Me and drink. He who believes in
Me, as the Scripture has said, out of his heart will
flow rivers of living water."

—JOHN 7:37–38

Bless the LORD, O my soul,
And forget not all His benefits:
Who forgives all your iniquities,
Who heals all your diseases,

Who redeems your life from destruction,
Who crowns you with lovingkindness and
    tender mercies,
Who satisfies your mouth with good things,
So that your youth is renewed like the eagle's.
                              —PSALM 103:2–5

The poor shall eat and be satisfied;
Those who seek Him will praise the LORD.
Let your heart live forever! . . .
All the prosperous of the earth
Shall eat and worship;
All those who go down to the dust
Shall bow before Him,
Even he who cannot keep himself alive.
                              —PSALM 22:26, 29

"Come, eat of my bread
And drink of the wine I have mixed."
                              —PROVERBS 9:5

"Ho! Everyone who thirsts,
Come to the waters;
And you who have no money,
Come, buy and eat.
Yes, come, buy wine and milk
Without money and without price.
Why do you spend money for what is not
    bread,
And your wages for what does not satisfy?
Listen diligently to Me, and eat what is good,
And let your soul delight itself in abundance."
                              —ISAIAH 55:1–2

"You shall eat in plenty and be satisfied,
And praise the name of the LORD your God,
Who has dealt wondrously with you;
And My people shall never be put to shame."

—JOEL 2:26

Now when one of those who sat at the table with Him heard these things, he said to Him, "Blessed is he who shall eat bread in the kingdom of God!"

—LUKE 14:15

For this reason I bow my knees to the Father of our Lord Jesus Christ, from whom the whole family in heaven and earth is named, that He would grant you, according to the riches of His glory, to be strengthened with might through His Spirit in the inner man, that Christ may dwell in your hearts through faith; that you, being rooted and grounded in love, may be able to comprehend with all the saints what is the width and length and depth and height—to know the love of Christ which passes knowledge; that you may be filled with all the fullness of God.

—EPHESIANS 3:14–19

■ God Can Give Them the Benefits of Belief Too

But as many as received Him, to them He gave the right to become children of God, even to those who believe in His name: who were born, not of blood, nor of the will of the flesh, nor of the will of man, but of God.

—JOHN 1:12–13

"Most assuredly, I say to you, he who hears My word and believes in Him who sent Me has everlasting life, and shall not come into judgment, but has passed from death into life."

—JOHN 5:24

There is therefore now no condemnation to those who are in Christ Jesus, who do not walk according to the flesh, but according to the Spirit.

—ROMANS 8:1

Blessed be the God and Father of our Lord Jesus Christ, who according to His abundant mercy has begotten us again to a living hope through the resurrection of Jesus Christ from the dead, to an inheritance incorruptible and undefiled and that does not fade away, reserved in heaven for you, who are kept by the power of God through faith for salvation ready to be revealed in the last time.

—1 PETER 1:3–5

But now Christ is risen from the dead, and has become the firstfruits of those who have fallen asleep. For since by man came death, by Man also came the resurrection of the dead. For as in Adam all die, even so in Christ all shall be made alive.

—1 CORINTHIANS 15:20–22

And you, being dead in your trespasses and the uncircumcision of your flesh, He has made alive together with Him, having forgiven you all trespasses, having wiped out the handwriting of requirements that was against us, which was contrary to us. And He has taken it out of the way, having nailed it to the cross.

—COLOSSIANS 2:13–14

Offering the New Life to Others, Through My 'Walk'

"Let your light so shine before men, that they may see your good works and glorify your Father in heaven."

—MATTHEW 5:16

To the weak I became as weak, that I might win the weak. I have become all things to all men, that I might by all means save some. Now this I do for the gospel's sake, that I may be partaker of it with you. Do you not know that those who run in a race all run, but one receives the prize? Run in such a way that you may obtain it.

And everyone who competes for the prize is temperate in all things. Now they do it to obtain a perishable crown, but we for an imperishable crown. Therefore I run thus: not with uncertainty. Thus I fight: not as one who beats the air. But I discipline my body and bring it into subjection, lest, when I have preached to others, I myself should become disqualified.

—1 CORINTHIANS 9:22–27

Now thanks be to God who always leads us in triumph in Christ, and through us diffuses the fragrance of His knowledge in every place. For we are to God the fragrance of Christ among those who are being saved and among those who are perishing. To the one we are the aroma of death leading to death, and to the other the aroma of life to life. And who is sufficient for these things? For we are not, as so many, peddling the word of God; but as of sincerity, but as from God, we speak in the sight of God in Christ.

—2 CORINTHIANS 2:14–17

For this reason we also, since the day we heard it, do not cease to pray for you, and to ask that you may be filled with the knowledge of His will in all wisdom and spiritual understanding; that you may walk worthy of the Lord, fully pleasing Him, being fruitful in every good work and increasing in the knowledge of God; strengthened with all might, according to His glorious power, for all patience and longsuffering with joy; giving thanks to the Father who has qualified us to be partakers of the inheritance of the saints in the light.

—COLOSSIANS 1:9–12

Walk in the Spirit, and you shall not fulfill the lust of the flesh. For the flesh lusts against the

Spirit, and the Spirit against the flesh; and these are contrary to one another, so that you do not do the things that you wish.

—GALATIANS 5:16–17

This I say, therefore, and testify in the Lord, that you should no longer walk as the rest of the Gentiles walk, in the futility of their mind, having their understanding darkened, being alienated from the life of God, because of the ignorance that is in them, because of the hardening of their heart; who, being past feeling, have given themselves over to licentiousness, to work all uncleanness with greediness.

But you have not so learned Christ, if indeed you have heard Him and have been taught by Him, as the truth is in Jesus: that you put off, concerning your former conduct, the old man which grows corrupt according to the deceitful lusts, and be renewed in the spirit of your mind, and put on the new man which was created according to God, in righteousness and true holiness.

—EPHESIANS 4:17–24

For you were once darkness, but now you are light in the Lord. Walk as children of light (for the fruit of the Spirit is in all goodness, righteousness, and truth), proving what is acceptable to the Lord.

—EPHESIANS 5:8–10

And do this, knowing the time, that now it is high time to awake out of sleep; for now our salvation is nearer than when we first believed. The night is far spent, the day is at hand. Therefore let us cast off the works of darkness, and let us put on the armor of light. Let us walk properly, as in the day, not in revelry and drunkenness, not in licentiousness and lewdness, not in strife and envy. But put on the Lord Jesus Christ, and make no provision for the flesh, to fulfill its lusts.

—ROMANS 13:11–14

For we have spent enough of our past lifetime in doing the will of the Gentiles—when we walked in licentiousness, lusts, drunkenness, revelries, drinking parties, and abominable idolatries.

—1 PETER 4:3

Therefore, since we have this ministry, as we have received mercy, we do not lose heart. But we have renounced the hidden things of shame, not walking in craftiness nor handling the word of God deceitfully, but by manifestation of the truth commending ourselves to every man's conscience in the sight of God.

—2 CORINTHIANS 4:1–2

In all things showing yourself to be a pattern of good works; in doctrine showing integrity, reverence, incorruptibility, sound speech that cannot be condemned, that one who is an opponent may be ashamed, having nothing evil to say of you.

—TITUS 2:7–8

But sanctify the Lord God in your hearts, and always be ready to give a defense to everyone who asks you a reason for the hope that is in you, with meekness and fear; having a good conscience, that when they defame you as evildoers, those who revile your good conduct in Christ may be ashamed.

—1 PETER 3:15–16

Offering the New Life to Others, Through My Words

Now all things are of God, who has reconciled us to Himself through Jesus Christ, and has given us the ministry of reconciliation, that is, that God was in Christ reconciling the world to Himself, not imputing their trespasses to them, and has committed to us the word of reconciliation. Therefore we are ambassadors for Christ, as though God were pleading through us: we implore you on Christ's behalf, be reconciled to God.

—2 CORINTHIANS 5:18–20

Then the eleven disciples went away into Galilee, to the mountain which Jesus had appointed for them. And when they saw Him, they worshiped Him; but some doubted.

Then Jesus came and spoke to them, saying, "All authority has been given to Me in heaven and on earth. Go therefore and make disciples of all the nations, baptizing them in the name of the

Father and of the Son and of the Holy Spirit, teaching them to observe all things that I have commanded you; and lo, I am with you always, even to the end of the age." Amen.

—MATTHEW 28:16–20

John answered and said, "A man can receive nothing unless it has been given to him from heaven. You yourselves bear me witness, that I said, 'I am not the Christ,' but, 'I have been sent before Him.' He who has the bride is the bridegroom; but the friend of the bridegroom, who stands and hears him, rejoices greatly because of the bridegroom's voice. Therefore this joy of mine is fulfilled. He must increase, but I must decrease. He who comes from above is above all; he who is of the earth is earthly and speaks of the earth. He who comes from heaven is above all. And what He has seen and heard, that He testifies; and no one receives His testimony. He who has received His testimony has certified that God is true. For He whom God has sent speaks the words of God."

—JOHN 3:27–34

"But you shall receive power when the Holy Spirit has come upon you; and you shall be witnesses to Me in Jerusalem, and in all Judea and Samaria, and to the end of the earth."

—ACTS 1:8

To them God willed to make known what are the riches of the glory of this mystery among the

Gentiles: which is Christ in you, the hope of glory. Him we preach, warning every man and teaching every man in all wisdom, that we may present every man perfect in Christ Jesus. To this end I also labor, striving according to His working which works in me mightily.

—COLOSSIANS 1:27–29

■ Proclaiming with Boldness

The Example of Peter

Peter, standing up with the eleven, raised his voice and said to them, "Men of Judea and all who dwell in Jerusalem, let this be known to you, and heed my words. For these are not drunk, as you suppose, since it is only the third hour of the day. But this is what was spoken by the prophet Joel:

'And it shall come to pass in the last days,
    says God,
That I will pour out of My Spirit on all flesh;
Your sons and your daughters shall prophesy,
Your young men shall see visions,
Your old men shall dream dreams.
And on My menservants and on My
    maidservants
I will pour out My Spirit in those days;
And they shall prophesy.
I will show wonders in heaven above
And signs in the earth beneath:
Blood and fire and vapor of smoke.

The sun shall be turned into darkness,
And the moon into blood,
Before the coming of the great and notable day
    of the LORD.
And it shall come to pass that whoever calls
    on the name of the LORD shall be saved.'

"Men of Israel, hear these words: Jesus of Nazareth, a Man attested by God to you by miracles, wonders, and signs which God did through Him in your midst, as you yourselves also know—Him, being delivered by the determined purpose and foreknowledge of God, you have taken by lawless hands, have crucified, and put to death; whom God raised up, having loosed the pains of death, because it was not possible that He should be held by it. For David says concerning Him:

'I foresaw the LORD always before my face,
For He is at my right hand, that I may not be
    shaken.
Therefore my heart rejoiced, and my tongue
    was glad;
Moreover my flesh also will rest in hope.
Because You will not leave my soul in Hades,
Nor will You allow Your Holy One to see
    corruption.
You have made known to me the ways of life;
You will make me full of joy in Your presence.'

"Men and brethren, let me speak freely to you of the patriarch David, that he is both dead and buried, and his tomb is with us to this day. Therefore, being a prophet, and knowing that God had sworn with an oath to him that of the fruit of his body, according to the flesh, He would raise up the Christ to sit on his throne, he, foreseeing this, spoke concerning the resurrection of the Christ, that His soul was not left in Hades, nor did His flesh see corruption. This Jesus God has raised up, of which we are all witnesses."

—ACTS 2:14–32

The Example of Paul

Then Paul stood up, and motioning with his hand said, "Men of Israel, and you who fear God, listen: The God of this people Israel chose our fathers, and exalted the people when they dwelt as strangers in the land of Egypt, and with an uplifted arm He brought them out of it. Now for a time of about forty years He put up with their ways in the wilderness. And when He had destroyed seven nations in the land of Canaan, He distributed their land to them by allotment. After that He gave them judges for about four hundred and fifty years, until Samuel the prophet. And afterward they asked for a king; so God gave them Saul the son of Kish, a man of the tribe of Benjamin, for forty years. And when He had removed him, He raised up for them David as king, to whom also He gave testimony and said,

'I have found David the son of Jesse, a man after My own heart, who will do all My will.'

"From this man's seed, according to the promise, God raised up for Israel a Savior—Jesus—after John had first preached, before His coming, the baptism of repentance to all the people of Israel. And as John was finishing his course, he said, 'Who do you think I am? I am not He. But behold, there comes One after me, the sandals of whose feet I am not worthy to loose.'

"Men and brethren, sons of the family of Abraham, and those among you who fear God, to you the word of this salvation has been sent. For those who dwell in Jerusalem, and their rulers, because they did not know Him, nor even the voices of the Prophets which are read every Sabbath, have fulfilled them in condemning Him. And though they found no cause for death in Him, they asked Pilate that He should be put to death. Now when they had fulfilled all that was written concerning Him, they took Him down from the tree and laid Him in a tomb. But God raised Him from the dead.

"He was seen for many days by those who came up with Him from Galilee to Jerusalem, who are His witnesses to the people. And we declare to you glad tidings."

—ACTS 13:16–32

■ Encouraging with Gentleness

Brethren, if a man is overtaken in any trespass, you who are spiritual restore such a one in a spirit of gentleness, considering yourself lest you also be tempted. Bear one another's burdens, and so fulfill the law of Christ.

—GALATIANS 6:1–2

Now we exhort you, brethren, warn those who are unruly, comfort the fainthearted, uphold the weak, be patient with all.

—1 THESSALONIANS 5:14

Brethren, if anyone among you wanders from the truth, and someone turns him back, let him know that he who turns a sinner from the error of his way will save a soul from death and cover a multitude of sins.

—JAMES 5:19–20

Index

Old Testament

Genesis

1:27–31	78–79
3:1–18	12–13
9:18–25	43
18:19	23
19:30–36	43–44
37:5–8, 11–14, 18–24, 28–30	9–10
47:11–12, 14, 23, 25a	5–6
50:17–20a, 21	53

Exodus

3:1–6, 10–11	82–83
6:6	6
13:8	23
22:22–23	27
23:12a	146

Deuteronomy

4:9–10	24
6:6–9	25–26
11:19	24
31:6	64
34:10–12	83

Joshua

1:1–8	67–68
1:9	65

1 Samuel

2:27–34	28–29
18:2, 10–11	42
20:30–34	42

2 Samuel

13:1–2, 6–14, 19	40–41
22:30	146

Job

2:7–9	69
2:10	69
3:2–13	87–89
4:14	61
6:2	72
16:6	72
30:27	61
33:8–9	13
35:2, 13	13
5:18	50

Psalms

1:1–3	133–34
3:5	148
4:4	66
4:4–8	148–49
6:7	72
8:1–9	79–80
10:12–18	27–28
10:14	73
18:2–6	44–45
30:1–5	69–70
22:1–11, 19	59–60
22:23–24	61
22:26, 29	166
23:1–6	115–16
25:8–11	100
27:1–5	6–7, 49
27:3	63
28:7–8	116
31:13	63
31:19–20	117
32:1, 6–8	87
32:3–5	105

34:4	46
34:4–5	86–87
37:23–24	107
38:4, 8–11	67
38:8	61
39:7–8	104
44:15	70
46:1–3	45, 116–17
46:2	63
51:1–2	104
55:22	45
59:10, 16–17	118–19
62:12	119
68:5	vii, 29
69:19	70
71:1	70
71:1–3	117
71:12–19	156–57
77:8–9	119
78:1–8	24–25
79:8	119
86:5	119
91:1–4	116
91:14–16	107
91:15	46
92:1–4	160
94:19	148
96:1–2	160
100:5	119
103:2–5	108, 165–66
105:1–4	136–37
106:1–3	160–61
107:1–2	161
107:21–22	161
107:31, 41–43	118
111:1–10	161–62
119:11, 16, 42, 50, 105	134
121	156
121:5–8	158
130:1–6	131–32, 164
139:1–16	113–14
139:14–16	114–15
142:1–4	164–65
145:1–12, 21	162–63
147:1–3	50

Proverbs

1:33	64
3:5–6	87
3:24	48
4:12	146
5:1–21	101–3
6:20	35
6:27–33	103
7:6–22	151–52
9:5	166
23:15–16	35
23:24–26	35
23:29–35	100–101
26:12	14
27:6	149
27:9–10	149–50
29:17	24

Ecclesiastes

2:24	148

Isaiah

1:6	38
5:21	14
21:4	61
26:3	141
40:1–4	10–11
40:29–31	146–47
43:1–2	48
43:1b–7	34–35
51:7	64
53:1–12	15–17
53:3–4, 10	72–73
54:4	70, 86
55:1–2	166
1:1–3	47
61:7	71, 86
63:16	30
64:6	14
64:8	29
66:13	29

Jeremiah

10:19	38
15:18	39

17:8	*141*	**Joel**		
30:16–17	*51*	2:26	*167*	
39:17–18	*46*	2:26–27	*71, 86*	
Lamentations		**Jonah**		
2:11–12	*39*	3:10	*65*	
3:32	*73*	4:1–2, 3–9	*65–66*	
Ezekiel		4:10–11	*66*	
34:11–16	*49–50*	**Zephaniah**		
		3:5, 8–19	*18–20*	

New Testament

Matthew			
4:1–4, 8–11	*80–81*	**Luke**	
5:11–12	*90–91*	9:57–62	*133*
5:16	*169*	10:38–42	*4–5*
5:22	*66–67*	11:5–10	*131*
5:27–30	*98*	11:33–36	*96*
6:14–15	*51*	12:1–5	*93*
6:25–34	*62*	12:5	*63*
7:9–11	*30*	12:7	*64*
8:23–24	*149*	12:32	*64*
10:29	*30*	12:32–34	*153*
10:37–39	*132*	14:15	*167*
11:28–30	*46, 132, 165*	15:4–7	*105–6*
13:43–44	*84*	15:11–24	*106–7*
13:45–46	*84*	16:15	*14*
13:47–49	*84*	18:9–14	*97*
16:26	*81*	18:20	*36*
18:1–7, 10–14	*22–23*	22:46	*135*
18:15–17	*150–51*		
18:21–22, 33	*53*	**John**	
18:21–35	*51–52*	1:1–4, 11–14	*120*
20:1–15	*17–18*	1:12–13	*167–68*
23:23–28	*95–96*	3:27–34	*174*
26:26–28	*139–40*	4:21–24	*137*
28:16–20	*173–73*	5:24	*168*
		6:27, 32–35, 51–58	*140–41*
Mark		6:35–40	*123*
4:35–41	*11*	7:37–38	*165*
6:30–32	*146*	8:12–14	*123–24*
12:1–10	*39–40*	9:41	*14*
12:41–44	*152–53*	10:7–18	*124–25*

10:24–38	120–21
11:21–26	125
12:25	81
14:6	122
14:23–26	126–27
14:27	142
15:1–7	125–26
15:18–25	89
16:5–15	127
16:20–22	47–48
16:33	46, 142

Acts

1:8	174
2:14–32	175–77
4:12	122
7:52–59	5
10:35	32
13:16–32	177–78
17:22–30	112–13

Romans

8:1	168
8:1–14	128–29
8:14–22	33
8:26–27	129
8:26–28	136
8:31–39	85
8:38–39	118
9:33	71, 87
12:1	147
13:11–14	98–99, 155, 171–72
14:7–6, 12–14, 17, 21	153–54

1 Corinthians

6:19–20	147
9:22–27	169–70
11:26	141
11:27–32	103–4
14:33	142
15:3–4, 12–20, 51–55	74–75
15:20–22	168

2 Corinthians

1:1–10	48
2:14–17	170

4:1–2	172
5:18–20	173
5:18–21	11–12
5:21	122
6:18	30
10:3–5	143
10:17	14

Galatians

1:4	122
4:3–7	33–34
5:16–17	154, 170–71
5:19–21	94
6:1–2	178–79
6:14	82

Ephesians

1:3–6	31–32
2:1–9	8
2:4–9	32
2:8–9	132
2:14–15, 17	142
3:14–19	167
4:17–23	155
4:17–24	171
4:25	151
4:26	67
5:3–7	94–95
5:8–10	171
5:9–10	155
5:21–33	26–27
6:1–3	36
6:4	26
6:11–18	143–44

Philippians

1:21	138
2:5–16	54–55
3:7–14	138–39
3:20–21	147
4:6	136
4:7	142

Colossians

1:9–12	170
1:27–29	174–75
2:6–10	139
2:9	120

2:13–14	*169*
2:20	*81–82*

1 Thessalonians
5:11	*150*
5:14	*150, 179*
5:17	*135*

2 Thessalonians
3:16	*143*

1 Timothy
1:12–16	*163–64*
2:1, 8	*135–36*
2:3–4, 9–10	*7*
6:6–11	*153*

2 Timothy
1:7	*63*
3:16–17	*133*
4:18	*48*

Titus
2:7–8	*172*
3:4–6	*7–8*

Hebrews
2:14–18	*122–23*
4:12–16	*93–94*
4:14–16	*157–58*
10:25	*150*
12:2	*71–72*
12:5–11	*99–100*
13:15	*135*

James
1:22–25, 27	*138*
2:2–8	*97–98*
5:13–18	*134–35*
5:19–20	*179*

1 Peter
1:3–5	*168*
1:6	*73*
2:5	*32*
2:19	*73*
2:19–23	*53–54*
3:12	*135*
3:15–16	*173*
4:3	*156, 172*
4:7	*135*
4:12–19	*90*
5:8	*143*

2 Peter
3:9	*105*

1 John
2:15–17	*79*
3:1	*30*
3:4–9	*95*
4:8–19	*30–31*
4:18	*64*
5:4–5	*79*
5:7	*126*

Revelation
7:9–17	*75–76*
11:15	*82*
14:7	*137*
15:4	*137*